IN THE LAST few years, polarized with regard social positions. *The Politics of Jesus* gives the reader a different perspective of how Jesus looks at the political issues of immigration, identity politics, marriage, and discrimination. Charlie Tuttle brings a fresh, powerful perspective on the political views of Jesus, the disciples, and the kingdom of God. He gives the reader context and history on the divisive issues facing believers. This is a book written for the issues facing America, but the lessons contained within it reach across humanity. I recommend this book as a must-read!

—REV. DR. SAMUEL RODRIGUEZ
PRESIDENT, NHCLC/CONELA
HISPANIC EVANGELICAL ASSOCIATION
WWW.LATINOEVANGELICALS.COM

Once I began reading *The Politics of Jesus*, I became so intrigued I could hardly put it down. Charlie Tuttle may challenge some of your preconceptions about politics and religion, but this is not a book written to validate or vindicate any political position. Current cultural and political issues have become polarizing, even among Christians. If you are seeking biblical perspective and would like to know if Jesus has contemporary observations and instructions about immigration and sexual identity, etc., the *Politics of Jesus* is a must-read.

—ALTON GARRISON
ASSISTANT GENERAL SUPERINTENDENT
THE GENERAL COUNCIL OF THE ASSEMBLIES OF GOD

The Politics of Jesus defines, designs, develops, and delivers a unique and consistent thread that engages you historically, emotionally, and factually. Charlie Tuttle has created an incredible push-pull format that will strengthen the resolve of the evangelical to focus on the rigid requirements of Jesus as it pertains to being a disciple. At the same time, it opens the mind of the unconvinced to the idea that the parables of Jesus are a glimpse into His reality. I am thrilled that at a time of such divide this unique literary endeavor will be a bridge of hope and provide room for one more thought, one more glimpse, and one more look at the One who knew "why" and not just "how."

—KRISH DHANAM
CORPORATE GLOBAL ADJUNCT
RAVI ZACHARIAS MINISTRIES,
MANAGING PARTNER SKYLIFE SUCCESS

There is a far worse spiritual condition than "the blind leading the blind"; it is the bland leading the bland! Reverend Charles Tuttle, in *The Politics of Jesus*, pungently reveals to the reader "the political back story" and the "personal inside story" of why Jesus did what He did in order to shake the known governments of His day. When you read this powerful book, you will move past the blindness of not knowing and the blandness of not caring to the brilliance of compounding impact throughout the rest of your life!

—DR. JAMES O. DAVIS
COFOUNDER, BILLON SOUL
FOUNDER, CUTTING EDGE INTERNATIONAL
GREATER ORLANDO AREA, FLORIDA

The Politics of Jesus is more than just a book; it is a reminder of a way of life in the once-upon-a-time America that has been diluted, disintegrated, grossly abused, and sold out—all under the auspices of American politics twenty-first-century style. Charlie Tuttle's research into the politics of this Jesus that we love and serve was a revelation to the fact that He is "intimately acquainted with all my ways" (Ps. 139:2). This book confirms and affirms to me that every aspect of our lives matter to Him, especially politics. *The Politics of Jesus* is a powerful description of the buzz words (WWJD) that appeared in the 1990s—epitomizing to this "politically-correct" culture the very foundation that makes the church, the church, a saint, a saint, and Jesus Lord of it all. It is still about His sacrifice, the truth, His grace, and the redemption of all humankind to know the truth that will set us free. This book is engaging, sound, and convicting. We are *not* Democrats, Republicans, or Independents; we are Christians!

—Judy Jacobs
Worship Leader, Pastor, Mentor, and Author
Dwelling Place Church International
Cleveland, TN

We must have answers to combat the noise of the culture. In a day when wrong is right, right is wrong, and truth is the new hate speech, it was time for someone to take up the mantle and write a message of truth to bring distinction to Christianity. In Charlie's book, we rediscover the true message of the Messiah Jesus brought to the world.

Charlie has written a book that is a plumb line to the church and nation. *Get this book! The Politics of Jesus* is a generational message of truth! This book will be a classic in the library of every person who desires a spiritual reformation and a textbook for those choosing to stand their holy ground. I say, "Bravo, my friend! Thank you for being willing to write such a powerful message."

—Patrick Schatzline
International Evangelist and Author
Remnant Ministries International

In *The Politics of Jesus*, Charlie Tuttle makes several important points in cleverly worded turns of phrase such as "Jesus was not an insurrectionist; he was a resurrectionist!" I appreciate his focus on the heart of the matter when he says, "Jesus did not authorize an uprising, but rather a prayer meeting." Speaking of the disciples, Tuttle writes, "Jesus did not supply them with power to rebel, but instead with power to reveal that Jesus is the Son of God." While I do not agree with everything in the book, I join Tuttle in his focus on unity in Christ across our political differences. He says, "It's not about seeking the same government; it's about seeking the same God." Expect to be challenged, surprised, and encouraged to faithfully follow Jesus.

—Bruce B. Miller
Senior Pastor, Christ Fellowship
McKinney, TX

In *The Politics of Jesus,* Charlie Tuttle brings a fresh, relevant understanding to the complicated political issues facing America and Christ-followers. The current geopolitical climate can be very hostile toward truth, especially biblical truth. But using reason, historical facts, and Scripture, Charlie enlightens the reader to understand the political tension that existed among the twelve disciples and the response of Jesus toward this tension. *The Politics of Jesus* confronts the divisive issues America is dealing with. It gives an insightful perspective on how Christ-followers need to engage the culture on tough political issues. This is a book you've been waiting for.

—Rob Ketterling
Lead Pastor
River Valley Church
www.rivervalley.org

THE
POLITICS
OF
JESUS

CHARLES TUTTLE

CREATION
HOUSE

THE POLITICS OF JESUS by Charles Tuttle
Published by Creation House
A Charisma Media Company
600 Rinehart Road
Lake Mary, Florida 32746
www.charismamedia.com

Unless otherwise noted, all Scripture quotations are from the Holy Bible, New Living Translation, copyright © 1996, 2004, 2007. Used by permission of Tyndale House Publishers, Inc., Wheaton, IL 60189. All rights reserved.

Scripture quotations marked NKJV are taken from the New King James Version®. Copyright © 1982 by Thomas Nelson. Used by permission. All rights reserved.

Scripture quotations marked THE MESSAGE are from The Message: The Bible in Contemporary English, copyright © 1993, 1994, 1995, 1996, 2000, 2001, 2002. Used by permission of NavPress Publishing Group.

Good News Translation® (Today's English Version, Second Edition) Copyright © 1992 American Bible Society. All rights reserved.

Design Director: Justin Evans
Cover design by Kenneth McClure

Visit the author's website: www.charlietuttle.org

Library of Congress Cataloging-in-Publication Data: 2016944691
International Standard Book Number: 978-1-62998-566-4
E-book International Standard Book Number:
978-1-62998-567-1

First edition

16 17 18 19 20 — 987654321
Printed in the United States of America

This book is dedicated to four men
who have impacted my thinking and
thought processes with their insight
and perspective; they cultivated within
me a passion for honest, accurate
communication, and they influenced my
life through strategic, sound wisdom:

My father, Jerry Tuttle
My grandfather, Charles Henry
My father-in-law, R.E. "Dick" Messner
My pastor and mentor, Alton Garrison

Your faithfulness to God and
to those in your life has forever
changed my life. Thank you!

CONTENTS

FOREWORD

M Y HEART WAS incredibly stirred as I read *The
Politics of Jesus* by my friend, Pastor Charlie
Tuttle. Why? Because today we are living in
the most divisive and deceptive time in the history of the
world. We must have answers to combat the noise of the
culture. In a day when wrong is right and right is wrong
and truth is the new hate speech, it was time for someone
to take up the mantle and write a message of truth to bring
distinction to Christianity. In Charlie's book, we find
out exactly what the true message of the Messiah Jesus
brought to the world. Just as the Apostle Paul did when
he stood in defense of the gospel on Mars Hill, this book
was written to say, "Jesus did not come to declaw human
nature; He came to dethrone it." The reader will experience a no-nonsense message of truth, fact, and prescrip-
tion! The apologetics involved in this book bring spiritual
reasoning to the most crass observer and empowerment to
the weariest of spiritual soldiers. Charlie takes the reader
on a journey to understand not only the political life of
Christ, but also what He had to deal with even amongst
His chosen twelve.

This book is a right-now message! America must have a
Holy Spirit awakening. We have been, for over 250 years,
the brightest light to the world. We are known as the
shining city on a hill. Nevertheless, our light is growing
dim. The world is looking to us for answers and many

wonder, "What has happened to our nation?" It is simple:
we have devalued life, turned Christianity into a voting
bloc, and persecuted truth!

We must realize that our nation and culture did not
change overnight. They changed when holiness became
odd, and much of the church decided it would be offensive to declare truth! Jesus never deemed political correctness to be the love language of the church! The confused
look on the face of a dying nation can be understood in
the reflection of its eyes as it now looks upon a land that
has removed truth.

We must awaken to the values of Jesus lest we dance our
way into the history books of forgotten nations. In fact,
I truly believe that the recipe of a fallen nation consists
of legalizing perversion, outlawing holiness, and over-
seeing the desolation of values and the criminalization
of distinction. The compass of a nation is the church of
Jesus and His followers. The compass is demagnetized and
destroyed when we have decided that we no longer serve
a just God. Instead, we have turned Him into a religious
relic of yesterday's morals.

Charlie has written a book that is a plumb line to the
church and nation. *Get this book! The Politics of Jesus* is a
generational message of truth! This book will be a classic
in the library of every person that desires a spiritual reformation and a textbook for those choosing to stand their
holy ground. I say, "Bravo, my friend! Thank you for being
willing to write such a powerful message."

As the late Dr. Martin Luther King once stated with
deep conviction, "Our lives begin to end the day we
become silent about things that matter." Dare we say to
our kids that our nation was destroyed because we who
had a voice decided the price to speak was more costly
than their freedom? The day of hiding in our places of

worship and hoping our love will permeate our walls into the community is over. This could be the church's greatest hour...We must all have a Revelation 3:19–20 moment: "Those whom I love, I rebuke and discipline. Therefore, be zealous and repent. Listen! I stand at the door and knock. If anyone hears My voice and opens the door, I will come in and dine with him, and he with Me" (MEV). That is, unless we too would rather continue to dance in the ballroom of demons while the devil parlays the next generation of a lost and dying world.

—Patrick Schatzline
International Evangelist and Author
Remnant Ministries International

INTRODUCTION

A FEW YEARS AGO while driving home from the office, I heard the voice of the Holy Spirit whisper these words to me: "Teach on the politics of Jesus." In an instant, that phrase froze in my mind as it was embedded in my heart. Until that moment, I had never heard of, thought about, or contemplated anything about the politics of Jesus.

Now, you have to understand: I am a political junkie. I follow politics like ESPN follows sports. Politics reflects culture, and culture reflects faith. Politics represents cultural evolution, transformation, and trends. It is the voting voice of the tipping point. Politics encompasses more than an electorate. It begins and ends with an electorate, but there is so much in between. However, I do not politicize the pulpit at our church, so I had never considered teaching on the politics of Jesus.

My immediate response to this nudge from the Holy Spirit was "Sure, this will be easy." Then I began to think through the words of Christ. I had just spent the previous twelve months reading only the four New Testament Gospels of Matthew, Mark, Luke, and John. I read through these four Gospels voraciously, and once I finished reading them, I picked up a different translation and started over again. It's the only Scripture I read for twelve months! I felt fairly confident that I could teach a series on the politics of Jesus. I thought I knew what Jesus would say if He were addressing American politics. Unknowingly, my world was about to get rocked.

As a political conservative and a person with a biblical worldview, there are times I struggle with national politicians, community leaders, and pundits embracing liberalism or even social progressivism while waving the flag of Christianity, quoting Scripture, and embracing the identity of a Christ-follower. To me, these people appear as political opportunists who use the Bible and the words of Jesus for their own political inclinations. After all, how can a God-fearing, Bible-reading, Christ-follower support abortion, gun control, or big government? How can someone be willing to sell out their American culture for open borders, applaud gay-marriage, support Palestinian causes, and claim to be a disciple of Jesus? How can someone be a strict, uber-environmentalist and claim Christianity?

My own questions caused me to ask different questions, deeper questions. What if this teaching series actually validated those "other" positions or undermined my political persuasions? Can something be biblical and not conservative? What if the teachings of Jesus conflicted with my personal politics? Now, obeying this nudge and teaching on the politics of Jesus didn't seem like a good idea at all. Honestly, it was uncomfortable to think my personal political philosophies could be at risk from greater biblical clarity.

The Scriptures reveal extreme tension between the disciples and their political ambitions.

After studying Jesus and His political interaction, I began to focus on His selection of the disciples. That's when more definition on this subject began to appear and the scriptural interaction of the disciples became obvious. The Scriptures reveal extreme tension between the disciples and their political ambitions. They did not see Jesus as a savior. They viewed

Jesus as a political separatist who would one day restore the dignity of the Jews and monarchial rule within Israel.

The disciples saw Jesus as an easy ticket to fame and special privilege; He would cause a transition of power from the oppression of Rome and the Jewish religious class to a new ruling class. They believed Jesus came to change the world instead of saving humankind. Their world, which needed to change, consisted of an occupied Jewish state. They saw what they wanted to see and heard what they wanted to hear. They were confident Jesus would break the yoke of Roman oppression. Jesus would open the market-driven tendencies of a theocratic citizenship. What could be better politically for the twelve than to be attached to Jesus?

Honestly, it was through studying the twelve disciples and the responses of Jesus to them that I learned the most about the politics of Jesus. Re-examining the instances where Jesus engaged and disengaged from people, issues, topics, and opportunities painted a magnificent masterpiece of a Savior not cheapened or threatened by the political rule and philosophy of His day. Although the disciples had political motivations, Jesus remained pure.

Studying the politics of Jesus drove away my political interpretation of the Bible, which was the faulty default switch of my theology. The politics of Jesus pummeled and lacerated my stereotypes of the disciples. I clearly understood their ambition and how it brought frustration to Jesus.

Jesus walked the fine line of wisdom by not opposing Rome while embracing a sovereign kingdom ideology. He embraced sinners, delivered prostitutes, cast out demons, and shared real life parables while confronting and correcting spiritual ignorance among His own disciples and religious overreach by the Pharisees and Sadducees. Jesus was kingdom focused, and His kingdom was not of this world.

The politics of Jesus opened my eyes to the process of

political ideology and its development. Let me explain. Most conservatives interpret politics and political philosophy through Judeo-Christian values or their personal faith. Values and faith are the funnel and filter for most conservatives. If issues cannot pass through, be attached to, or co-exist with their values or faith, then it is not a viable political philosophy.

Most liberals or progressives, on the other hand, separate their politics from their faith. They politically embrace one philosophy or idea without it conflicting or compromising their faith. Their faith is only faith. Their political view may or may not agree with their faith. My liberal friends are comfortable compartmentalizing their faith and keeping it separate from their politics.

Another huge distinctive between conservatives and liberals, progressives, and tea partiers is the role of government in society. A conservative is shaped by Judeo-Christian values or faith more than a liberal. This means a conservative typically views big government as a threat to faith and religious freedom. Liberals have a different perspective.

A liberal tends to see faith and religion as separate from the government and politics. They do not want to corrupt their faith or religion by infusing it into government. Faith and religion is to be experienced in the church and government is to be experienced in society. A liberal typically views government as the great equalizer.

Conservatives perceive faith as something that unites; liberals perceive faith as something that divides.

A conservative sees society as their social mission; a liberal sees society as their social community. Conservatives perceive faith as something that unites; liberals perceive faith as something that divides. Tea-party conservatives want less government for the sake of liberty, and progressive liberals want more government for the sake of fairness.

After studying the disciples, it was apparent Jesus intentionally selected disciples we would label today as progressive, liberal, conservative, tea-party, independent, or libertarian. Jesus, for the most part, allowed political, economic, and vocational tension to exist between the disciples. He rebuked them for their open-air arguing, private agendas, and misapplications of His teaching. Many times, He addressed their issues through His silence. Jesus gave them room to be who they were because He called them as they were.

As you read this book, realize this is not a clean, bow-wrapped discussion. It's like humanity—somewhat messy, but embodying a message.

This book is not written to validate or vindicate any political position. It's written to give the reader perspective on political and ideological patterns through the life of Jesus. It's written so you can determine spiritually where you stand on some important issues facing America. Believe it or not, your personal, political decisions and persuasions influence the future destiny of the greatest nation and civil community known to humankind.

The principles in this book reach across cultures and other forms of global government. But the examples, illustrations, and applications are made in the USA. This book is about understanding Jesus, not conforming to political talking points. This book embraces biblical discovery.

It's my hope that, as you read each page, you will allow the thoughts to stand on their own as you develop your own perspective. Your thoughts, ideas, and responses may differ from what's written—and if so, that's fantastic! My desire is that, through reading this book, you discover your own thoughts, convictions, and persuasions on political issues so you can intelligently articulate and express those thoughts to others.

Beyond that, the intent is to engage your understanding and position regarding the kingdom of God. Let me explain. The last portion of this book explains the difference between the two divine kingdoms Jesus referenced most: the kingdom of heaven and the kingdom of God. I think these are two separate, distinct kingdoms. The first belongs to the saint, and the second belongs to the Spirit. One is for the now realm; the other is for the next realm. One is for the manifestation of my faith; the other is for the manifestation of my hope. Jesus taught kingdom principles, and those principles speak to a heavenly government, a kingdom government, created and centered in perfection.

Until His kingdom appears, Christ-followers are foreigners, non-citizens, aliens on this earth. This doesn't preclude our political involvement, but it should put it into perspective. There is no perfect earthly form of government, which is why we need to work to continually improve our government, while placing our hope in God.

Before concluding these thoughts, I want to thank my incredible wife, Sherri, for supporting me, encouraging me to write this book, and tolerating the excessive schedule conflicts of writing, pastoring, traveling, and leading our family. I want to thank our adult children, Gentry, Weston, and Payton for discussing the contents of this book with me and challenging my thoughts. A special thanks goes to my staff, our church Board of Directors, and the incredible congregation of Genesis Church for supporting the process of transferring a pulpit series into a manuscript. I also want to thank my publisher for believing in this idea. Mostly, I want to thank my Lord, Jesus Christ. This belongs to You, Jesus, not me.

I trust you enjoy *The Politics of Jesus*.

BEST WISHES,
—CHARLES TUTTLE

Chapter 1

A DOSE OF PERSPECTIVE

W HEN OUR THREE children were young, we watched many animated movies. One of my favorite scenes comes from the 2007 Disney Pixar movie, *Ratatouille*. The setting is France, and the story features a rat named Remy and a chef named Linguini, who cooks sauces and soups at Gusteau's Restaurant.

Remy has a big dream, and that dream is to be a chef. Remy has only one problem. He's a rat, and rats are not allowed in restaurant kitchens. Linguini also has a big dream of owning his own restaurant. There is only one problem: Linguini is a terrible chef and is all thumbs in the kitchen. He's never cooked much of anything. He is very uncomfortable in the kitchen. However, Remy the rat gives Linguini the ability to cook by directing him from atop his chef hat.

Because of Remy, Linguini is becoming a renowned Paris chef, famed for his incredible soup and dishes. This cartooned adventure only gets more tense as "Ego," the renowned Parisian food critic, walks into Gusteau's for a bite to eat and a culinary review. Ego is one of the main "villains" in the movie. He is the most austere food critic in Paris. His reviews cause restaurants to either flourish or fail. Now, on a night when nothing seems to be going right in the kitchen, Ego steps inside Gusteau's Restaurant.

Mustafa, the waiter, recognizes Ego as he is seated. The scene begins with Mustafa gathering his courage to speak

with Ego. Mustafa is nervous and experiences an immediate loss of confidence. Mustafa knows the kitchen is
struggling. He tries to hide his nervousness as he draws
a deep breath, gathering courage to approach Ego's table.
Mustafa walks up and greets Ego. Ego's head is buried
in the menu. When Mustafa inquires as to what Ego would
like to order, Ego replies with an apparent tone of conde-
scension that he is craving a little perspective.

Mustafa is confused. Ego then snaps the menu closed
and, sounding more definite this time, requests some
"well-seasoned perspective." Mustafa remains baffled. He
timidly inquires again about Ego's menu selection. Ego's
response is still focused on perspective. Mustafa is looking
bewildered, trying to determine what dish on the menu
Ego is wanting.

So Ego replies something like this, "If you'll provide the
food; I'll provide the perspective."

This is by far one of my all-time favorite moments in
any movie, whether animated or, as my kids used to say,
"Made with real people." This exchange captures a great
value in life: that value is perspective. Perspective brings
accuracy to life. In the absence of perspective, the future
can become very deceptive. In our modern era, one of the
traits most lacking in our culture is accurate perspective.

So, if you as the reader will permit, let's begin with a
good dose of perspective. As you read this chapter, you
may see the last four decades very differently or perhaps
somewhat similarly. Obviously, my perspective is only
that, and it's somewhat personal. Your perspective may be
completely different, which is fine.

The goal is to give a childhood to adulthood perspec-
tives on culture shifts. Let's look at cultural shifts like
race relations, political correctness, voter identity, social
engineering, re-gendering, modern social-justice theology,

and a few other issues. Turn the pages and join me on a journey that has been half a century in the making.

THE WORLD OF MY CHILDHOOD

Sometimes, I miss being a kid. The world of my childhood was comfortable, uncomplicated, and predictable. Boundaries were clear, and violations were obvious.

As children, we didn't deal with racism, income equality, transgender issues, the underserved, situational ethics, the environment, or a host of other current political issues and ideologies. Even though these things may have existed in the adult world, we were just kids. In our world, we had words like *white people, black people, rich people, poor people, bullies, goof-offs, weirdo's, freaks, hippies, girlie-boys, teacher's pet, yes sir, no ma'am,* and *it depends.*

Mostly, we had rules and structure. We didn't have "time-outs" for contemplation; our parents did not count from one to three before moving toward us to administer discipline. They usually moved as quickly as we did, and if by chance, we did get away, we received spankings, groundings, or both when they caught us! Discipline was administered with an expectation of immediate behavioral and attitude change!

In our world, there was no such thing as tolerance. Anytime we said a word that was offensive or crude, Mom was there to wash our mouths out with soap. Kids in the neighborhood didn't care about skin color, origin, race, or ethnicity. We had no clue about the existence of things like prejudice, racial tension, white privilege, discrimination, micro-aggressions, sex education, or feminism. We cared about the deeper values of life like catching a ball, running faster, swinging a bat, riding skateboards, racing bikes, throwing snowballs, or building a fort. We grew up thinking it was pretty normal for Anglos,

African-Americans, and Hispanics to play together because that was our life.

We had gender-specific games, roles, and toys. Girls played with dolls or make-believe kitchen appliances; boys played sports or with toy guns. As boys, we would shoot each other with imaginary bullets and make real-life sound effects ourselves; we'd *pow, pow, pow,* and then fall dramatically to the ground as if we were meeting our Maker. After a few dramatic fake deaths, we'd take a gun battle break to drink Kool-Aid® and down a cupcake. We played dead; we played army; we played cops, robbers, and zombies. We played rock music, competing in outrageous air-guitar and air-drum battle contests. Candy cigarettes were cool, and baseball cards were better than money. Yep, sometimes I miss those days.

At recess, we played hard. After school, we played even harder. We didn't have video games, hand-held devices, social media, selfies, or Instagram. We had bus-stop challenges and dares. At school, we had real playground equipment that required physical activity, imagination, and competence. Monkey bars and slides were the stuff legends were made of.

The school cafeteria served ice cream, and we could bring a can of soda in our own cartoon-covered lunch box. Individually wrapped candy or gum was traded undercover at recess or passed under the desks in the classroom, like some made-for-TV movie drug deal. There was no food patrol, nutrition czar, or sugar-police.

We were just kids growing up, having fun and stirring up trouble. We made paper airplanes, paper footballs, and paper finger-folders that had mystery words written on the inside of each fold. The holder of the finger-folder counted through a numerical code, a rhythm, or recited a poem that caused a mystery word to appear. Most everyone believed in a silly kind of way that whatever word was written on the finger-folder would definitely come true. Boys were called boys, and girls were called names because they carried cooties. Honestly, we never saw a cootie or even knew what one looked liked; we just knew girls had them, and boys didn't. At times, I sort of miss those days.

What made those days special were not just the silly games, crazy imaginations, and sugar laced soda pop. Rather, it was growing up with simple boundaries, understandable rules, and common community values. It was knowing that most people were alike in most ways, even though we were different. Schooling consisted of an education in the basics of reading, writing, history, science, geography, and math. People respected religion, even if they did not have any. People could reasonably expect help from a stranger, if help was needed. Life was less complicated, and people were generally less stressed and more easygoing. People took the time to laugh, relax, and celebrate others. There was a protective value placed on people and a sharable value placed on stuff.

The current reality and consistent fear of danger from random gun violence, school shootings, abductions, molestations, or harm from strangers did not exist in our neighborhood. Sure, there were bad people like Charles Manson and others, but in most communities across America, people were decent, upright, and helpful to their neighbors. People just seemed kinder; I miss those times.

Even though people disagreed on politics, religion, and other matters, it wasn't divisive or coercive. People engaged in genuine debates absent of labels, names, and vitriolic responses. No matter what the debate or disagreement was about, once it was discussed, it was over, period. People who didn't see eye to eye could still laugh together, eat together, and care for one another. Disagreement didn't seem to cause division.

The country had some serious issues like civil rights, the Vietnam war, Watergate, and protests on college campuses. Divorce was a reality for some of the unfortunate marriages. Desegregation was a reality for public schools and institutions. Drugs, sexual promiscuity, rock-n-roll, and teenage smoking were cultural concerns to parents, teachers, and clergy.

However, the country was also headed toward new adventures and discoveries like landing on the moon, building a lunar rover, and completing the next phase of Disneyland. People had more decency than less, and issues were not perceived as personal; they were just issues. Majority votes decided most controversies and commonsense was a common value. Courts focused on justice, not fairness. People knew right from wrong and good from bad.

Those were the carefree days when summer vacation started before Memorial Day and the day after Labor Day marked the return of public schooling. Tests had correct and incorrect answers, and homework was part of academic training. No one knew what ADHD or ADD or OCD was, and no one cared. Some kids just had more energy than others, and some kids just needed more discipline. Right or wrong responses to behavioral issues could be debated at length, but one thing was certain…kids were label-free, and behavior modification medications were uncommon. It was a great time to grow up in America.

CHANGING TIMES

Something changed while growing up, learning to drive, going off to college, marrying my college sweetheart, and starting a family. Life sped up, values shifted, and society evolved. We advanced from copiers to fax machines, from personal computers to the internet—and now to the cloud. We progressed from wall phones to cell phones to smart phones. We once held hands; now we hold handheld devices. We've progressed from shopping catalogs to malls to Amazon.com; now cyber-delivery systems and drones are the future of retail delivery. Former core business sectors have ceased being core business sectors; some have ceased being businesses completely. They are just a part of capitalistic history. People have come to expect real-time news and financial information, immediate trades on Wall Street and an app to handle personal banking, shopping, parenting, and home utilities. But that's not all that has changed in America.

Citizens have been transformed from Americans to political labels, demographics, and special-interest groups. While exercising the individual right to vote, we have become a voting bloc, a statistical data point of predictability based upon race, gender, profession, income, and county of residence. While living as individuals, we have been categorized as a political statistic and posted as a colored icon on a political map.

In almost every area of consumerism, weekend shopping experiences have become research data for marketing and advertising firms. Mailing addresses, emails, phone numbers, and consumer preferences have been collected and proffered to companies, only to be recategorized and repurchased. Calculated assumptions developed privately from our life data have been pushed publicly through the media as the new norms.

Media labels have been placed on Americans. The labels have been generated from the entertainment programs we have watched or downloaded, the cable, radio and satellite stations we have listened to and the articles and information we have read from specific news sources or websites.

Within the span of a rather short lifetime, voter dispositions and political leanings have been calculated through
lifestyle patterns, purchases, recreational interests, annual
income, place of residence, race/ethnicity, and a few other
data points. In all of this, we have been completely ignored
as individuals.

The battle for the citizen's voice to be heard has risen
to new levels of tension and frustration. Political money
has become our biggest competitor against pure democracy. Thanks to Congress and the Supreme Court, bundled
money has now become a viable political voice. Big money
in politics has devalued and extended the voice of constitutional free speech beyond the voter. Theoretically, it seems
to have replaced free speech. It's a scary precedent when the
influence of a non-living, non breathing entity can advance
into the political process and rival the voter's voice.

Think about this for a moment: the constitutional right
of free speech has seemingly been competing with the
legal, political voice of money. U.S. currency has been a
debtor's note since the gold standard for currency was
abolished by FDR in 1933. Now currency is guaranteed
through citizen labor and taxable productivity. It's gotten
a little more twisted in American politics. Our Founding
Fathers fought against the system we have created.

Justice has become based on the outcomes for the
"greater good," rather than on facts or truth. Situational
ethics and philosophical fairness have set up strongholds
that influence decisions in business, education, entertainment, justice, and government. The rules have changed
from justice to fairness, from fairness to awareness.

Societal demand is placed on the capacity to understand instead of the ability to decide. Tolerance is the
political doctrine most used by those who are most
intolerant. Political correctness is neither a value nor a

principle. Political correctness is a process to undermine and intimidate the will of the majority through invoking unapproved privileges to the minority.

Something else has happened over my lifetime that has never happened over the lifetime of any other generation in the history of America. People have become data points, DNA samples and voter classes. We have become trackable, traceable, and taxable.

Our usefulness in the political system appears to have been reduced to choosing electable personalities based upon cable news sound bites and pundant opinions. The real selection of political leadership seems to reside within the media, PACs, and lobbyists. In many ways, our electoral choice has not been a true representation in government, but rather the lesser choice of evils in a corrupted political environment.

Honestly, that brings up what many have missed most in this country. We miss being regarded as real people. We are not a political voter bloc, a racial demographic, or an economic class. We have not become haters, dividers, race-baiters, or political scoundrels because our values align differently. We have worked hard to become contributors because we value our citizenry. We have participated as real people who vote because we care about our country and its future. We are not Republicans, Democrats, Independents, conservatives, or liberals; we have been and will always be Americans.

A SALTLESS WITNESS

America and Americans have become more and more polarized by politics. But not just Americans—Christians have become polarized as well. The divide between political philosophies threatens spiritual unity, community, and cohesion within the body of Christ. Unified political philosophy seems more cherished than biblical expression or doctrinal accuracy among Christ-followers. As the modern American church pivots toward political acceptance instead of biblical significance, it is laying the foundation for secular persecution based upon a saltless witness.

As the church loses its peculiar voice in culture, it becomes an unnecessary leech sucking away community resources through the special privileges associated with tax exemption and religious freedom. When the church acquiesces away its moral voice and spiritual compass within the local community and nation, acceptance of sin replaces conviction from righteousness. Once the distinguishing message of truth and grace embodied in the ministry of Christ is rejected by the church, the message of the gospel becomes a life-hindering embarrassment, and not a life-saving message.

As the modern American church pivots toward political acceptance instead of biblical significance, it is laying the foundation for secular persecution based upon a saltless witness.

Currently, in some religious circles, spiritual dialogue is being infused with emotional personal attacks and political correctness. What's more alarming is the inclusion of Christian philosophy, doctrine, and teaching to support and bridge political chasms. In this postmodern culture, theological conclusions are based upon the acceptance of strategic, emotive conclusions instead of scriptural interpretation and understanding. Political sides are preselected, then biblical verses, examples, or principles are selectively applied to position the argument as God-blessed or biblically permitted.

SECULAR CHRISTIANITY

Science and scientific theory have replaced the authority and truths of scripture among many believers. Modern anti-God theories broadcasted across cable channels seem believable because they're visual, not because they're true. Many Christ-followers have been pulled into deceptive, humanistic theories. These theories have challenged the accuracy of scripture with little rebuttal. They have been accepted as truth due to the programming and influence of the History Channel, National Geographic Channel, Discovery Channel, and other media. Some believers have now questioned the authority of God and the reliability of the Scriptures because they do not know the scriptures or God's power.

Truth has now become second to perception, and situational ethics has created a conflicting worldview. Neo-absolutes have become nothing more than repackaged situational ethics based on humanistic philosophy rather than time-tested absolute principles. Scriptural accuracy and integrity has been lost among many believers amid the clamor for an open-minded faith. This open-minded faith has become nothing more than a tacit doctrinal application of open grace and enduring love that excludes eternal judgment.

In addition to all this, race, roots, and gender have become the presumed indicators of geo-political opinions and persuasions. Gender confusion-inclusion consumes the media as special-interest stories pivot the culture against religion. The media has placed extreme scrutiny and pressure on Christian organizations to adapt and adopt secular progressive values and celebrated dysfunctions. Some churches, spiritual leaders, and denominations have left the integrity of God's Word for cultural acceptance and celebration.

The pressure on American Christ-followers and faith systems to accept, approve, and encourage more deviant moral lifestyles and choices has become a progressive evolution of cultural reprobation. It appears as if compromise has been wrapped in tolerance for the express purpose of preserving a religious buoyancy, not religious freedom. This doctrine of compromise has become a leading value to some in the American church, much like Darwin's doctrine of natural selection is the leading value of evolution.

The current post-Christian American culture promotes a mantra that "a faith that is not neutral is a faith that is not safe."

Modern liberal theology endorses a loving, evolving, divine attribute instead of a living, eternal God. The authority of Scripture has come under great political pressure to conform to the culture of legal depravity and deviating social norms. Christ-followers have forgotten that historically the church has always been counter-culture.

The current post-Christian American culture promotes a mantra that "a faith that is not neutral is a faith that is not safe." Principle-centered faith has been referred to as extremism. The significance of Christ's humanity, deity, holiness, and sanctity has been lost in the morass of culturally, demonic doctrines.

Convictions have become controversial and opinions have become equally divisive. Political philosophy now defines friends, foes, and funding. And...as if it were not complicated enough, the name or values of "Jesus" added to any business, organization, or charity has created a venomous furor that has led to new levels of disassociation and attack.

Ravi Zacharias poses this question: "How do we reach a generation that listens with its eyes and thinks with its feelings?"[1] Not only is this a great question, but it also provides a great commentary to our current condition. As Americans, we have become so influenced by what has been seen and felt that we have exchanged thinking for feeling and truth for perception. Facts no longer lead to discovery of the truth. Many Christ followers have embraced the soulish instead of the spiritual. The church has exchanged God's truth for a cultural lie, and the consequence has become a backslidden condition.

Sadly, people have been evolving from situational ethics to situational theology. Many believe they possess truth within themselves, and they have looked for facts to support their inner truth. When facts do not support their truth, those facts have simply been rejected. We have placed ourselves above truth, and the result has been there is very little recognizable truth left in our society. When we as humans become our own absolutes, there are no absolutes. It's impossible to have over seven billion absolutes!

POLITICS AND RELIGION

In the decades of the 1980s and '90s, financial expansion and technological discoveries positioned America firmly as a world leader. Yet during this time, American evangelical Christians had been lulled into a spiritual coma by the aroma of success, the economic expansion of Wall Street, and the public success of conservative, religious voices. Many Christian leaders were overtly focused on spiritually cleansing the church instead of focusing the church to reach lost humanity.

From the late 1980s forward, many believers from the charismatic, evangelical, and Pentecostal circles wondered if the rapture of the church, or the catching away of believers from the earth, would occur during the September Jewish feast of Rosh Hashanah in 1988. This was the year of Israel's fortieth anniversary as a nation. Many pre-tribulation believers had theorized that this would be the year the Lord caught His church away. Tribulation clocks were prophetically set as these believers hoped and prayed for this event.

Many charismatic, evangelical, and Pentecostal churches preached the imminent return of Jesus. Songs of Christ's return were sung; new songs were written. Prophecy services, conferences, and books were common. Most American believers did not believe they would see the dawn of the twenty-first century.

However, after the disappointing no-returns of Jesus in 1988 and 1989, a new prophetic theory was embraced that believed Christ would rapture the church by the year 2000. Some of these hopeful believers huddled in devotion, worship, and prayer during each Rosh Hashanah from 1988 to 2000 for the expected return of Jesus. Yet, year after year, the unraptured hopeful emerged afterward with questions, confusion, and disappointment. Unfortunately, some of their children watched and experienced the same theological disappointment and doctrinal confusion.

These children were being taught in a subtle way that the promises of God were undependable, somewhat scary, and not realistic. These Christian parents and leaders were sincere in their faith, but sincerely wrong in their application of theology. Their good intentions were being undone by their zeal and their lack of scriptural understanding.

After surviving the many disappointments of a non-returning Jesus, Christ-followers embraced the position that they had more theological time before the Rapture. An unintentional reframing of faith had begun, accompanied by hollowed-out doctrine and shallow convictions.

It became popular to look the part while it became permissible to lack the substance of a devout Christ-follower. American Christianity was becoming a shadow movement. Many American churches in the late 1980s and early 1990s also transitioned away from core ministry principles and embraced professional business principles. Churches operated more like big business. Pastors were viewed as CEOs and congregants as stockholders. Churches began to shift from the body ministry model to a business ministry model.

A spirit of codependency became entrenched across much of the evangelical and charismatic landscape of America. Leaders invoked and testified of the move of God so the move of God could invoke and testify of these leaders. The excess of hubris replaced the humility of anointing.

Christian media and parachurch ministries were coming of age. The bright spotlights of television, radio broadcasting, specialized ministries, resources, and publishing created a huge conflict of interest among the faithful as to the matters of tithes, offerings, and financial gifts. Big ministry was coming "in," and it seemed the local church was going "out." Churches felt pressure to conform to the American image and the expectation of bigness—or risk closure. Big required new levels of resources and funding. Principles and convictions had limits, in part because ministries had huge operational bills, debts, and liabilities.

During this time, some very gifted leaders became spiritual sharks feeding with a carnivorous appetite of money, power, and influence. Spiritual voices spoke critically of one another, almost as if the failure of one voice guaranteed the success of another's voice. Not only did the message of the gospel become glamorous in its presentation, theological understanding was replaced by spiritually-relevant application. No longer would pastors risk their reputations on theological mysteries or doctrines when they could teach the application of broader, less controversial, life-relevant topics. Many churches became competitive with each other. Denominations were selective, separate, and sequestered. Sharp, religious contrasts developed. Christianity was faithfully mocked on programs like Saturday Night Live, by late night TV comedians, and by entertainers. Journalists did stories and hit pieces on the luxurious lifestyles, excessive materialism, and greed of pastors, evangelists, and ministries.

When Christians turned on one another, it fueled the media, courts, and public opinion to turn on them as well. Making it worse were faulty, well-publicized theological errors and moral failures. Numerous, erroneous theological predictions brought scoffing and public humiliation. Moral failures forced additional public correction, which in turn created more mocking.

Other theological positions called for the church to become a political kingdom and governmental force. Many sincere Christians registered as Republicans in order to "take back America" from White House scandals and disreputable activities. Some Christian voices decided the church needed to become a more ardent political force. Christians exercised their right to vote; politicians would either cater to religious values or be voted out of office. The religious right was coming of age in America.

The litmus test of this voting bloc appeared in the early 2000 elections, when George W. Bush was ushered into the presidency with the help of the evangelicals, the Supreme Court, and Florida's hanging chads. For the first time in forty-six years, religious conservatives controlled the House, the Senate, and the Presidency. Conservative Christianity was "in," and liberalism was on the run—or so it seemed.

America needed strong, political leadership from the president. But some Christians were demanding that the president be a righteous, political pastor-leader. The expectations of the religious-right stirred animosity and sarcastic abandonment from left-wing politicians and from the emerging youth culture. This forced key principles and values underground and out of the mainstream dialogue.

As religious, political leaders began to lead Washington, their humanity became more and more obvious. Extramarital affairs by those who ran on family values plagued D.C. Money scandals followed; ethics charges came after that. The spirit of conservative, evangelical corruption tarnished the Congress.

In 2006, a progressive San Francisco liberal named Nancy Pelosi asked the country to vote in a democratic majority so "we can drain the swamp of corruption."[2] Her appeal won over the American voters. The House of Representatives changed party control two years before the next presidential election.

JUNK FAITH?

During this same period of time, a new breed of churches, pastors, and congregants began to rise. Doctrinal distinctions began to fade as a new spiritual generation came of age. Sick of the spiritual materialism and the power grabbing of their childhood, these Christ-followers passionately blazed the trail of social justice and economic equality in the name of Jesus. Their mantra was the core of Matthew 25:35–40: "I was hungry and you fed me...naked and you clothed me" (GNT).

In the eyes of a new generation, Christianity had been corrupted by the complication of egos and logos. This

emerging generation wanted a simple Jesus, simple doctrines, and a simple faith. These simplistic-faith ideo-
logues brought a social consciousness back to American
Christianity that placed new value on the poor, the brokenhearted, and the needy. It was a social consciousness
that was desperately needed, but arguably may have been
mistakenly applied.

Yet, in all their biblical simplicity, this generation was
much more socially liberal than their parents. They were
not opposed to social drinking, sexual activity outside of
marriage, body piercings, and tattoos. Self-expression was
part of their mode of evangelism. They could look unchris-
tian, be tatted up or pierced, have an adult beverage, blend
into the culture, and still be a Christ-follower.

Living this oxymoronic witness gave these young
believers a unique sense of power and a ubiquitous source
of identity. They no longer needed organized church for
their faith. They needed a pervasive identity of action-oriented simplicity for their faith.

Lacking systematic, biblical theology, they identified
more socially with liberal progressives than their conservative parents. For the first time in American history, an
emerging Christian generation felt more welcomed and
comfortable outside the church than inside the church. They
have become the unchurched of the faith—fully present in
Christ and almost completely absent from church.

These action-oriented believers were strong toward tolerance and weak toward scriptural inerrancy. Life lessons
were learned from watching media, entertainment, and
video games. They added friends through networking tech-
nologies. Relationships shifted from actual to virtual to
on-demand; social values shifted as well. Scriptural values
were just outdated ideas contained within some faith-based

initiative or Sunday school class. Those things were old school, and this generation was creating new school.

Faith had become something that was experimental. Spiritual substance was to be more flexible than constrictive, more experiential than blindly accepted. Faith had to fit normal cultural abnormalities and family dysfunctions. Faith was becoming more socially complex and less individually convicting. Non-offensive tolerance was a more righteous value than offensive truth. Truth was based on perspective, not principle.

For many in this generation, their friends were gay, bisexual, or experimenting, including some of these young Christians. Abortion was considered by many to be an alternate form of legalized birth control. Natural drugs were accepted as part of life experience. Porn was the norm, and the topic of sexuality was over discussed; they had been discussing sex since fifth grade.

Many had been educated in more liberal-leaning, public schools from kindergarten through college. The majority had been raised in single-parent homes due to divorce. Their picture of commitment was a cell phone contract, not a marriage vow. This would become the first American generation raised to think and process decisions through a political lens instead of historical perspective.

This generation came to faith exposed to critical religious leaders and believers filled with judgmental backbiting. They watched religious and political leaders erase moral lines. They attended public schools and universities where their faith was scrutinized, and in some instances, abandoned.

They wrapped their faith around social activism and justice, which justified their faith. They became passionate, simplistic religious dissenters from enduring a lack of tangible, compassionate Christianity. Furthermore, they became spiritually confused watching Pentecostal, charismatic, and evangelical churches refuse to compassionately engage lost gay people because they were gay, not because they were lost.

This generation brought the American Church to a new crossroad. Perhaps for the first time since the Protestant reformer Martin Luther nailed the reformation thesis on the Wittenberg door, the attributes of God had been circumstantially applied against God's own standards. The result has become a form of godliness lacking the conviction, standards, holiness, and consistency of the very God they professed.

New theological boundaries have been formed. Some of these believers have accepted a viewpoint that the cross represents God's tolerance for sin, not the cleansing death of it. Their theology has morphed into divine acceptance from divine judgment. To these newly reformed believers, God's judgment has become a form of intolerance that cannot correctly fit into their politically correct faith.

Their gospel has now become conceptual, not literal. Sexuality has been humanized and has lost its sacredness. Purity has become disassociated with transformation.

Grace has become its own doctrine of tolerance. It's no longer a spiritual journey; grace has become an end to itself. Grace has to be accepted, even in the absence of life change. It has become the message of junk-faith, and only time will tell the true effect of its acceptance upon the world.

And as off base as the current religious, yet anti-God-wired world has become, it looks eerily congruent to the global culture Jesus was born into over 2000 years ago. Even though the issues have become adamantly different, the core philosophies driving those differences remain very consistent. Human nature hasn't changed much over time. Ideas regarding government, money, finance, education, social norms, and moral and ethical deviances remain similar no matter the culture, country, era, generation, or century.

For the American Christ-follower, the dish has been made, and now it's time to get some perspective.

Chapter 2

THE RESURRECTIONIST

O NE DAY THE scorpion had to cross the river, but the river was flooding and swift. It was too dangerous for the scorpion to attempt crossing. So the scorpion approached a frog, who was nestled along the bank of the river in the water.

The scorpion crawled onto a nearby rock and pleaded with the frog to ferry him across the river on his back. The frog refused. He said, "The river is swift and rough. If you are on my back, the water will splash on you and terrify you. Once you are terrified, you'll react and and attack me. Your stinger will poison me in the middle of the river, and we will both die. The answer is *no!* I will not swim you across the river."

But day after day, the scorpion sat on a stone near the swollen bank of the flooded river, asking the frog to give him a ride across the river. Each time the frog said "No!" and each time the scorpion promised he would not sting the frog. For weeks this went on, back and forth, every day until the frog began to wear down. He believed the scorpion was sincere and would not sting him. The scorpion had convinced the frog he was no threat, he just merely needed to cross the flooded river.

The next day the frog agreed to transport the scorpion on his back. The frog told the scorpion, "I'm going to trust you. You must trust me. I will not let you drown. When the water flows across my back and the waves strike your body, continue to hold onto me. No matter how scared you are or how rough the journey gets, *do not sting me, or we will both die!*" The scorpion calmly agreed and climbed on the back of the frog.

About halfway across the river, the water began to splash upon the scorpion. He lost his footing a few times and felt like he would be washed off the back the frog. Suddenly, a big splash from a wave hit the scorpion. He pulled his tail up and drove his stinger into the frog's neck. The frog screamed out in pain as his body began to burn from the poison. He asked the scorpion, "What have you done? Why have you stung me? Now your poison will paralyze my body, and we will both drown! I was your only hope to survive the river. Why did you sting me?" The scorpion replied, "I am so sorry I've stung you...you were right, the rushing water scared me. I just couldn't stop myself from attacking you...I'm sorry; it's just my nature."

That short parable really gives us perspective about life and human nature. Often people ask, "How does history consistently repeat itself?" The reason why history has a repetitive nature is simply that, although global cultures are uniquely different, human nature is uniquely consistent. A two-year-old in India acts very similar to a two-year-old in Indiana. History may be influenced by culture, but it is driven by human nature.

In fact, human nature is a more consistent variable when it comes to duplicating similar circumstances over a lengthy period of time than culture itself. This is why Jesus could not deliver humanity with a human nature. If His nature lacked the fullness of deity, His mission would end in failure. Nothing gained, everything lost.

NO ORDINARY NATURE

The Book of John describes the nature of Jesus as the perfect blend of grace and truth. In fact, Jesus wasn't a blend of both; He was full of both…full of grace and full of truth. Two dynamic tensions resident in one being.

In the process of becoming empty, Jesus would challenge the very substance of His own fullness.

The humanity of Jesus was unlike any other human. His humanity would, in fact, interrupt the nature of all humanity. Jesus would reveal the whole deficit within all human beings by emptying out divine grace and truth in a brutal furor for all human sin. This would be no small feat. In the process of becoming empty, Jesus would challenge the very substance of His own fullness.

Only deity cloaked in humanity could be emptied at the great exchange on the cross. The frailty of the human flesh would consummate with death, diving into a divine exchange of life. The presence of Jesus on earth would be considered toxic by the leading professors of religion. Jesus would be a thorn to the political leaders answering to Rome and a scourge to the religious leaders who answered to the Jews. His words would challenge their political thoughts, and His teachings would defy their religious dogma.

But His actions, full-blown with grace and full-throttled in truth, would silence all His religious foes and political critics. Their religious teachings, political doctrines, and cultural leanings would be shown to be insufficient, imperfect, and corrupt. All the while, His divine nature and attributes would be tested through death and vindicated through His resurrection from the dead.

NO ORDINARY TRUTH

Jesus just wasn't full of truth; He was (and is) truth. Jesus spoke words which created a new reality of truth. For just a moment, imagine how this "truth attribute" must have functioned.

When Jesus told the woman caught in adulterous immorality, "neither do I condemn you; go and sin no more" (John 8:11, NKJV), those were not just words of compassion or relief. Those were words of truth. His words to her were not just human words based on human understanding or empathy. Jesus spoke eternal words in eternal truth as the source of all truth. Words spoken in everyday conversation from the lips of Jesus were just as powerful as words spoken at creation.

Everything Jesus did or said was either to reveal, confirm, or establish truth. His truth is so far beyond our realm of truth. Often, our human truth is comprised of discovering and interpreting facts. But for Jesus, His truth was comprised of delivering Himself, His thoughts, and His intent; everything within and from Jesus was truth. His mission was to empty Himself, or literally to empty His truth, upon humanity.

With Jesus, even simple, short phrases or sentences boomed truth across the canvas of humanity. In John 19:28 while He was dying on the cross, Jesus called out, "I thirst!" This was more than just a natural condition. The Bible states this was a prophetic sign entrusted to Jesus for that very moment of time. His statement of thirst would establish and confirm the true validity of divine prophecy recorded centuries earlier pertaining to His crucifixion.

The pivot point of such prophetic accuracy would be embodied in His integrity and entrusted to the spoken truth of Jesus. Jesus could not reveal Himself without confirming all the ancient, prophetic truths written about

Him. Truth was attracted and attached to Jesus—even if that truth was recorded centuries beforehand and consisted of a simple prophetic sentence.

The truth Jesus fully possessed was no ordinary truth. This was a truth so bold it bound the written Old Covenant of God to a spoken New Covenant from Jesus. His truth confronted the conscience and stirred the heart.

The truth of Jesus silenced the mouths of His critics. It embarrassed and emboldened those seeking to discredit and murder Him. His truth was so penetrating that His enemies pierced Him in revenge. Jesus spoke words so true the physical realm could only respond with submission or rebellion. Jesus shared the light of truth so bright it brought sight to the blind while assaulting and overpowering deceptive darkness.

Jesus was on a mission to restore the damaged entry portal of the kingdom of God to humankind. He was an extraordinary leader who cast a compelling kingdom vision embedded within eternity. This vision would demand His death and resurrection from the dead for the revelation to be seen by those closest to Him—and beyond them.

Yet His mission and vision would be misunderstood by those closest to Him and misinterpreted by those most critical of Him. Jesus claimed a kingdom, but not one in this world. Jesus was not seeking to overthrow an oppressive Roman government. His mission was to overthrow an oppressing human nature.

Jesus did not come to declaw human nature; He came to dethrone it. His passion was to not only live in truth, but to die in truth and offer Himself to God for all of humankind. *Jesus was not an insurrectionist; He was a resurrectionist!*

I've often wondered how much risk and faith were

involved for Jesus to bring a selected group of disciples around Himself. At the time Jesus called the disciples, He was like a rock star. People flocked to Him from the region. He would heal people, cast out demons, feed them, and teach them with compassionate authority.

Jesus was not just divine; He was congruent. His teaching demonstrated the very authority His life professed and revealed. His tongue, tone, and teaching were in harmony with Father God and the prophets.

Jesus was the perfect blend of passion and compassion, zeal and empathy. His traits were like those of great warriors, who could sustain themselves on determination and accomplishment alone. Jesus was able to deny Himself while meeting the temporal needs of those around Him. He carried the source of His anointing within Himself— an anointing that was from His heavenly Father.

Jesus was not dependent upon the affirmation or acceptance of others. His identity and self-acceptance was in His heavenly Father. He only modeled the actions of His heavenly Father. He only spoke what He heard His heavenly Father speak.

His divine nature was beyond humanity as much as His physical frame was beneath divinity.

Jesus was God incarnate, impassioned with His mission and zealous for His Father's will. His divine nature was beyond humanity as much as His physical frame was beneath divinity. But all of His essence and being was about to be put at risk by the company of twelve disciples; twelve myopic men who had somehow translated the ministry of Jesus into their own political agenda.

PERFECT CANDIDATES

Disciples were a common fixture in the Middle-Eastern culture. This culture was an active oral-learning culture. Many of the traditions and much of its history was handed down generationally through verbal lessons and conversations. The ability to read and write was the exception in the era of Jesus, not the norm. Therefore, disciples and scribes were significant contributors who passed forward oral and written history.

In the Jewish culture, disciples and discipleship had meaning. Disciples were not to be confused with followers, especially as it related to Jesus. There were significant differences between the two categories. Followers were many; disciples were few. Followers listened to Jesus's teaching; disciples learned to embody it. Followers came as crowds; disciples came as individuals or in small groups. Followers were curious; disciples were convinced. Followers brought their needs; disciples brought their resources. Followers gave a day to be with Jesus; disciples gave their lives. Followers stood by, but disciples sold out. Disciples possessed significance and purpose, especially if the disciples followed Jesus.

Calling disciples to Himself gave Jesus credibility and exposure in His culture. Yet beyond a message of credibility, disciples also represented continuity. The mere fact that others aligned themselves with a teaching or teacher typically guaranteed the teaching would continue.

In the culture and time Jesus was on the earth, disciples were expected to communicate and demonstrate what their teacher taught. Disciples gave context. They often helped people understand by giving additional explanations in the absence of the teacher.

Disciples displayed commitment. Disciples functioned as messengers, hosts, servants, and the event team.

Without a strong buy-in from disciples, a teacher was unable to host followers, speak to crowds, or manage his own security.

When Jesus selected His disciples, He chose men who were opposites to Himself and to one another. He appointed men who did not rubber stamp His ministry. In fact, most had to be convinced for themselves that Jesus was the Son of God.

These men were white, grey, and blue-collar workers. Some were very educated while others were not educated at all. Some had a very smooth, personable presence while others were completely unpolished and gruff. Most of the time, they did not agree among themselves. They argued with each other continually. They were socially and economically separate and had various levels of buy-in relating to Jesus and to each other.

The disciples were introverts and extroverts, business owners, government workers, and political hacks. Their only common point of connection was Jesus. Yet each of these men accepted an assignment that would completely expose their hearts and defy their political philosophies and convictions.

Their relationship with Jesus would challenge their allegiance to all their relationships, possessions, and achievements. Everything they pursued would be embodied or deconstructed as Jesus spoke these words: "The kingdom of heaven is like" or "The kingdom of God is like." They were spiritual novices, irreligious, and unattached to tradition. They were perfect candidates for the impossible.

Jesus taught them to pray using kingdom expression and priority. Jesus introduced them to kingdom philosophy and truth. He explained to them the difference between faith and unbelief.

RISKY BUSINESS

Taking on disciples was also a risk for Jesus. On a few occasions, the disciples lacked courage, and they were forgetful; many times they were stubborn. They always seemed to jockey for position or access to Jesus. They were convinced Jesus needed them, perhaps more than they needed Jesus.

Their discipleship mentality was position-oriented instead of servant-oriented. Even the mother of James and John approached Jesus requesting her sons have the predominate positions in the kingdom throne room. Instead of rebuking these two brothers or their mother, He invited James and John to journey with Him. He invited them to drink from His cup. They would later discover His cup was a cup of personal sacrifice and not a cup of prolific comfort.

While Jesus was introducing a greater kingdom than Rome, the disciples saw Jesus as the human accelerant of their political ambitions. The miracles of Jesus embodied their popular understanding of a Jewish Savior. He was compassionate, authoritative, and decisive. Simultaneously, there were pockets of a populist movement seeking to declare Jesus king by force. To a citizenry that was overburdened and undercompensated, Jesus was a perfect political solution.

The Jesus they saw aligned completely with their expectations of an energized political leader for a new Jewish State. To the disciples and followers of Jesus, the purpose of the Messiah was the political overthrow of Rome and the establishment of a revised Jewish nation. When Jesus spoke of being the Anointed One and the Messiah, the disciples assumed it was to establish a national political kingdom. They simply could not recognize the need for a personal Savior when their country needed to be revived and rebuilt.

> Their vision required Jesus be a political sur-
> vivor, not a personal Savior.

Perhaps to Peter and the others, fishing for men was a metaphor for rulership, governance, and power. Sitting on His cabinet and being part of His administration was an intoxicating ambition of the twelve. So much so, that when Jesus spoke of His death, Peter rebuked Jesus. Their vision required Jesus be a political survivor, not a personal Savior.

The disciples struggled to embrace and understand a messianic mission focused on the eternal salvation of people. According to Jewish prophetic traditions, the Messiah was about political upheaval, the overthrow of oppression, and the restoration of David's kingdom over Israel. The disciples had no doubt Jesus was going to break the yoke of Rome. His purpose was somehow their purpose, and His miracles only promulgated a political coup de grace against the occupation of Roman oppression.

BLINDED BY NATURE

For almost three years, these disciples misunderstood or misinterpreted the meaning of miracles, teaching moments, and acts of compassion. They missed the bold truths tucked into the entertaining stories and parables told by Jesus. When they did capture a spiritual truth, it was as if they stumbled upon it or fell into it. They walked daily with the Creator of the universe and struggled to see His passion for the lost people created in His image. But honestly, they could not help but be blind to all of it; after all, it was just their nature.

After researching the disciples, it would seem somewhat understandable that they could miss the missional impact of Jesus. But what about our generation? How is it that we are missing the true mission of Jesus Christ? After all, we have the advantage of experiencing salvation through Jesus by believing in His Lordship. We have the advantage of possessing and reading the Scriptures, which reveal and direct us to Jesus Christ. We have access to the body of Christ, manifested through the local church. We have Christian media, music, conferences, trips, and tours of the Holy Land. How is it that we are just as detached from the mission of Jesus in this generation as the disciples were in their generation?

As we fast forward into the twenty-first century and look at the people who claim to be Christ-followers and disciples, there is a real disconnect to Jesus. Honestly, I have struggled with the public claims of some who profess Christ. These iconic figures who have made a open profession of Christ embrace a lifestyle that violates Scripture. They claim their faith in Christ supports a lifestyle that is not separate from the world.

Watch any entertainment awards show like the Emmys or the Grammys, etc., and most of the entertainers produce a product of filth and worldliness while giving thanks to God and adorning themselves with jeweled crosses. It reminds me of the song I learned as a child watching Sesame Street: "one of these things just doesn't belong here." Something doesn't fit this brand of Christianity, and very few Christ-followers seem concerned. It's as if believers have never read 1 John 3:4–6:

> Everyone who sins is breaking God's law, for all sin is contrary to the law of God. And you know that Jesus came to take away our sins, and there is no sin in him. Anyone who continues to live in him will not sin. But anyone who keeps on sinning does not know him or understand who he is.

Watching contemporary society claim the promises and grace of Christ caused me to ask these questions:

- How could people who claim to be Christian affiliate with political causes and platforms that contradict the Bible?

- How can believers endorse lifestyles or relationships that Scripture warns us to avoid?

- How can believers embrace Christ while supporting a political candidate or party philosophy that seems anti-faith?

- When a believer's politics collide with the Bible, how can they defend their politics through their faith and the Bible?

These questions brought on more questions.

- How can Christ-followers read the same Bible, follow the same Savior and have differing political opinions and interpretations of truth?

What about issues like:

- Pro-life versus pro-choice?

- National security versus war?

- National debt versus social programs?

- Legislative morality versus personal liberty?

- Traditional marriage versus same-sex marriage?

- Birth gender versus transgender?

- Natural gender identity versus gender neu-
  trality or elective gender identity?

- Nature steward versus radical
  environmentalist?

How could Christ-followers have the common bond of
the Holy Spirit, the Holy Bible, and a renewed mind—and
yet remain divided on political issues? The answer to this
dilemma is found in the Bible. It pivots around the people
Jesus selected as His disciples.

Chapter 3

THE TWELVE DISSIDENTS

C HOOSING TWELVE DISCIPLES from the hundreds of followers was like a game of roulette. Given the prophecies regarding the ministry of Jesus and the length of time Jesus knew the candidates, the chances of selecting the right people were somewhat limited. So Jesus prayed thoroughly through the night and, from that moment forward, He selected the twelve and never looked back.

Think about this process for a moment. Jesus was selecting twelve men to journey with Him as He moved toward the cross. The cross was the ultimate will of God, the purpose for which Jesus came to the earth. This was a critical mass moment in the history of Jesus, and it would determine the legacy of His suffering, death, burial, and resurrection. There were no do-overs. This was a "one and done" selection for Jesus. He had to get this right.

These twelve men would be attached to the ministry of Jesus forever. Prophetically, one of them would have to betray Jesus; one would have to deny Him; all of them would have to abandon Him. There were no personality tests, no strength finder assessments, no spiritual gifts tests, and no criminal background checks. There was no human resource department. It was just Jesus and the leading of the Holy Spirit. This was more than faith alone; it was courage, risk, and sovereignty colliding together for a divine purpose.

At this point in time, Jesus was leading a populist movement. His teachings, miracles, and authority placed Him
right at the top of the messianic ballot. People loved Him,
and Jesus was not afraid of the religious establishment.
Jesus challenged the religious leaders publicly. He asked
questions which they were ambitious to hear but reluctant
to answer. Jesus would not back down. The more they were
offended at Jesus, the more He would offend them. Being
selected as one of His disciples carried some "oomph"
with it. Jesus was a rabbi with no equal, so it would seem
His criteria for the disciples would be very similar.

> The prayer was no sooner prayed than it was
> answered. Jesus called twelve of his followers and
> sent them into the ripe fields. He gave them power to
> kick out the evil spirits and to tenderly care for the
> bruised and hurt lives. This is the list of the twelve
> he sent: Simon (they called him Peter, or "Rock"),
> Andrew, his brother, James, Zebedee's son, John, his
> brother, Philip, Bartholomew, Thomas, Matthew,
> the tax man, James, son of Alphaeus, Thaddaeus,
> Simon, the Canaanite, Judas Iscariot (who later
> turned on him).
>   —MATTHEW 10:1–4, THE MESSAGE

Using today's current terminology and understanding
of American politics, let's identify some of the disciples
based upon their political leanings and tendencies. To do
this, let's look at the meaning of their names, their occu-
pations, other evidences from the New Testament era, and
their relationship with Jesus and each other. Obviously,
their political dispositions relating to Israel or Rome
were very different from the social issues facing us today.
However, there are some real similarities between the disciples and the conservative, independent, liberal, and progressive ideologies and practices of today. (Please note

these are designations for understanding. There is no way anyone can place social positions on these designations. However, it does give us a general understanding of their cultural, political persuasions and how those persuasions relate to current American politics.)

Peter and Andrew: Think classic, small-business Republicans. They were passionate business owners, running and growing the family fishing business. They had boats, nets, and employees. Peter understood managing and leading, not just fishing and boating. This is probably one of the many reasons Peter was attracted to the leadership, teachings, and miracles of Jesus.

Peter and Andrew most likely demonstrated an obnoxious contempt towards taxation and big government policies. They lived and fished in the region of Galilee, which was quite famous for its anti-Rome sentiment. Rome was no friend to the Jews, especially in the northern region of Israel. Demographically, it was less political than Jerusalem. Ideologically, it was a beehive of disdain for Rome. It was the poor side of Israel; taxes and poverty did not mix well with the constituents.

Peter appears to be the tightwad of the twelve. Remember, it was Peter who didn't offer to pay his own voluntary temple tax in Matthew 17:24–27. Directed by Jesus to cast a single hook into the water, catch a fish, and pull a coin out of the fish's mouth seemed like an unusual way to provide tax payment.

Peter did as Jesus directed and was probably relieved when Jesus miraculously paid the tax for both of them. It may have been that Jesus wanted to show Peter that a business and a business professional blessed by God could provide most anything, even a tax payment. It was a lesson on provision Peter would not forget.

Peter and Andrew worked hard to make a living, owning

their own family business. It was so special to them that, after the resurrection of Jesus, they both returned to fishing (John 21:3). With only intermittent appearances of Jesus after His resurrection, it seems as though the fresh air, the spray of the water, and weighty pull from fish in their nets was indeed the perfect life for them. Their freedom was on the Sea of Galilee.

On Galilee, Rome was no longer an oppressive government but a mostly forgotten reality. The open waters, the smell of the fish, and the feel of the nets in their hands refreshed and protected their souls. Rome had no right to their increase or their skills. On the waters of Galilee, Rome's oppression was impotent.

After the resurrection, Peter and Andrew were back in the fishing business—at least for a while, until one early morning when Jesus showed up on beach. As the aroma of grilled fish wafted into the air, a conversation could be overheard in the distance. As the fire crackled, a spark was relit inside of the heart of Peter. From that point on, the focus of the family business shifted again. As their nets were dried and mended, these fishermen began to imagine what it would be like to feed the little lambs of God. They set aside their boats so they could fish for the biggest catch of all—the human heart.

James and John: Think impressionable, idealistic, and impetuous; the classic youth vote. James and John were young opportunists seeking power and influence the easy way. Typical of a younger generation, they wanted the benefits without paying the price. Known as the sons of thunder, the cultural interpretation of their moniker actually meant sons of chaos; these were two very opinionated young men.

James and John recognized Jesus as an upcoming political leader and were most likely awed by their experiences with Him over the last thirty-six months. Jesus was a world-class leader, and they were passionate to spend as much time with Jesus as He would permit. This could be a reason why Jesus included them in a few private miracle experiences.

However, these brothers also appear to be instinctively positional in their political aspirations. They had been disciples of Jesus for almost three years, and as Jesus was getting ready to reveal Himself in Jerusalem, the brothers sent their mother to ask Jesus if her sons could "sit on your right hand and left hand in your kingdom." It was a very bold request and an intentional power play. These two places were the seats of honor and authority in Jewish culture.

With an unsophisticated, simple tone, Jesus asked the one question that would seal their destiny in the years ahead. Both Matthew 20:20–24 and Mark 10:35–40 detail the conversational exchange as Jesus inquires if they are willing to drink of His cup and undergo His baptism. Their response was an immediate, perhaps flippant or naive "yes" (which must have made their mother proud). Then Jesus told them that they would indeed drink from the same cup and undergo the same baptism. However, the positions they sought would be decided by "My Heavenly Father" who determines the seating arrangement in the kingdom.

The Bible states when the other ten heard their request, they became indignant! Can you imagine the angry, verbal response against James and John? Perhaps the other disciples were angry because they had not thought to inquire about the availability of these high positions. Whatever the reason, it was evident that their request created contention among the politically minded disciples.

Perhaps their real intent was addressed a few verses later in Matthew 20:25–28 when Jesus comments on how the rulers in the Roman government regarded positional

authority and titles of honor. His statement was basically this: "What you're observing in the Gentile government is not how My kingdom works. Greatness comes
from serving, not from being served." The words of Jesus
seemingly diffused the strife and directed their reflection
toward their own hearts.

Nonetheless, the real issue at hand was that James and
John had a positional, political mentality. They ascribed
to a philosophy that benefits and privileges should be
given to them because they wanted them, not because
they earned them. They were shrewd enough to get their
mother involved, and they were bold enough to go for the
best positions.

Whether or not you appreciate their tactics, you certainly have to appreciate their ambition. It would be this
same ambition that would cause John to outrun Peter on
the way to the tomb of a resurrected Jesus. There was some
competitive quality inside of John and James that always
drove them to be first.

John would always refer to himself as the one Jesus
loved. He writes this as if Jesus loved none of the other
disciples. No other gospel writer refers to John as the
beloved. But in his mind, John would not quit until he
became the one Jesus loved most. Perhaps it was his passion, his immaturity, or his lack of perspective, but in all
the interactions with the twelve, John was always seeking
to be in the front position.

Bartholomew: Think rigid, thrifty, safe conservative.
The Hebrew word-picture associated with his name literally means rigid and thrifty, one who accumulates.
Bartholomew is mentioned four times in the Scriptures;
every time he is mentioned in a group of people.

There are no standout moments, experiences, or actions
that can be attributed to Bartholomew. He seems like a

very dull person. It's possible he was an introvert, but his lack of action is what defines him, not his personality.

What is known about him is very minimal. He is not a risk taker, or a leader; he's just a disciple in the crowd. Bartholomew is only identified in a group and never by himself. He seemed to be the one who played it safe. Three of the four Gospel authors mention his name only once; Luke mentions that he participates in a prayer meeting in Acts 1:13.

Bartholomew seems to be the guy who shows up but does nothing else notable. We know he was present, and that's about it. This might explain the lack of results associated with his name. However, tradition holds he went into India, evangelized, and died as a martyr.

Thomas: Think independent or perhaps libertarian. Scripture portrays Thomas as a distrusting individual. Whether he is generally distrusting of people, of Jesus, or of the other eleven disciples is not clear. What is clear is that his disposition rides the line of negativity and doubt. He is the one disciple who seems to selectively gather with the other disciples when he chooses. He is occasionally outspoken, typically negative, and not easily convinced.

The other disciples identified him as Didymus, meaning twin or double. Perhaps "twin" is his nickname or just his identity. What's interesting is that Thomas seems to display characteristics associated with second-born individuals. These characteristics include tendencies to be more loyal, negative, and sarcastic, which certainly fit his profile.

He would be more of a "show me" individual, and less of an "I believe" personality. Confidence would not be a word used to describe Thomas. Perhaps his selective appearances with the disciples are actually associated more with procrastination than isolation. Scripture is unclear, and this is probably a moot point because both those tendencies are natural traits of second-born individuals.

In John 11, Thomas is the first to speak up that the disciples should go with Jesus to visit their deceased friend, Lazarus. At the same time, there is a specific death threat against Jesus in the same village where Lazarus is buried. While the other disciples are attempting to talk Jesus out of making the forty-minute trip, Thomas is the first to say "Let's go also that we may die with Jesus" (John 11:16).

It's hard to call that a faith-filled, loyal statement when the end result is a true doubt any of them will survive the trip. In fact, there could be a sense of sarcasm in his response. Nevertheless, Thomas was convinced even if the outcome was not survivable, supporting Jesus was honorable.

But most of all, Thomas is famous for his absence when Christ first appeared to the disciples after His resurrection. After missing the moment of seeing Christ, Thomas ignorantly declares, "I will not believe unless I see Him with my own eyes and touch His wounds personally." Eight days later, Jesus appears again to the disciples, and this time Thomas is present. Jesus looked at Thomas and said, "Don't be unbelieving, but believing" (John 20:24–27). This truly was an open rebuke to the doubting statements Thomas made just a week earlier. It was at this moment that the political independent would capture the nickname "doubting Thomas."

Distrusting and distant, Thomas remained selectively separate from the disciples. He too, would make his way toward India to preach the gospel alone. It was there in South India that he would invest his life, converting many and giving his life as a martyr.

Simon the Zealot: Think Tea-party conservative, rigid constitutionalist. The Zealots were a Jewish liberty movement.

They consisted of conservative Jews who held public gatherings, protests, and meetings to stir the people against Rome. Zealots were passionate, mostly non-violent conservatives who operated as an anti-Rome movement. Zealots believed in the exaltation and adoption of the original teachings in the Torah (the Jewish law), and they pushed for Jewish political independence and liberty from Rome. The best example of the zealots in American politics is groups who identify with the Tea Party. Scripture labels Simon as a zealot in Luke 6:15 and Acts 1:13; this movement was a major source of his passion, identity, and agenda.

Zealots were considered "the fourth Jewish philosophy" by Jewish historian Josephus. This recognition by Josephus, who did not empathize with their cause, shows how much the zealots ingrained their philosophy into the Jewish culture. They were purists as it related to the law. It is no wonder Simon was attracted to Jesus because Jesus came to fulfill the law and remove the oral traditions of religious teachers from its content.

Zealots despised Rome, taxes, and oppression as well as the people who supported or tolerated the Roman government. Simon most likely had a personal political agenda against those who did not support the Jewish law or an independent Jewish nation.

It's interesting to note that Barabbas, the criminal set free in exchange for Christ's crucifixion, was also a zealot. He was scheduled to be crucified by Rome because murderous violence occurred in one of his public protests. Barabbas was considered by Rome an enemy of the state. Simon would be viewed the same way, perhaps even more so.

Simon's grandfather, a man named Hezekiah, is considered the founder of the Zealots. He was executed by Herod in 46 BC. The execution seemed so unjust that the Sadducees sought Herod to be tried for his execution.

Simon's father was Judas of Galilee. He was killed in 6 BC, and his political activism and death is mentioned in Acts 5:37. Simon and his brother James continued the rebellion. Both were crucified in 46 or 48 AD.

The Jews were very careful how they engaged the zealots. The religious scholars known as Pharisees and the legal scholars known as the Sadducees had a love-hate relationship with the zealots. The Pharisees despised their strict interpretation of the law of Moses, but appreciated their passion to overthrow Rome. The Sadducees loved their passion for the strict interpretation of the law, but they prospered under Rome. Both groups were very careful to not side with the tactics of zealots.

The zealots based their political activity in the region of Galilee. Because Jesus Himself came from this area, there is a reasonable speculation that some of the zealots were very aware of Jesus. No doubt this was attractive to Simon.

Simon was a political lightening rod; he was a Roman rebel and a Jewish nationalist. Yet Simon had to assimilate with the other eleven disciples. He probably came into the twelve as an outsider. His presence among the twelve immediately created suspicion of Jesus and the disciples.

Simon probably carried a grudge against Rome for the deaths of his grandfather and father. He was a political dissenter, and his movement supported justifiable violence and uprisings. His political ideology never left his personal identity. A zealot he was, and a zealot he would be.

Simon probably infused political tension into the group dynamic of the disciples. Jesus took an incredible risk selecting Simon to be one of the twelve. This addition would undoubtedly create intense speculation about the intent and motives of Jesus from the onset. Religious leaders would be hesitant to embrace Jesus and suspicion from the Roman leaders would be abundant. In spite of the appearances,

Jesus selected Simon. But even more than that, can you imagine the tension between Simon and Matthew?

Simon and Matthew were political opposites, and in any other context may have been considered political opponents. Both were from the same area, and most likely had an awareness of one another. Yet whatever it was that attracted Jesus to Simon, something strongly similar must have attracted Jesus to Matthew. Jesus went to where Matthew was working to call him. This in itself sent a strong message to Simon that his political cause or personal preferences would not negatively influence or limit the focus of Christ's ministry. The calling of Matthew may have also reinforced that the kingdom message of Jesus was beyond national Israeli politics. No matter the motive or reasoning of Jesus, Simon would have to support the decision to include Matthew.

Matthew: Think big government liberal. As a tax collector, Matthew was considered a committed oppressor over his own people and a self-ordained opportunist. Rome meant big government, and big government meant high taxation, military occupation, and forced labor. As a tax collector, it was customary to inflate taxes to include a very generous, subjective collection-commission.

Rome was a government of excess, economic waste, progressive ideas, debauchery, idolatry, and moral collapse. However, Matthew probably considered the positives this oppressing government brought to Israel. It was Rome that built roads, bridges, and viaducts for water. Rome brought a secular government to Israel, instituted an empire currency, and carried out punishments for extreme crimes.

Rome had the strongest military of that era and expanding borders due to military conquest. Under Rome's rule, economic expansion and trade became the norm. Rome, for the most part, also allowed its subjects to maintain their cultural customs and practice their religion. The Jews considered Rome as both an oppressor and an occupier. Most Jews were unable to become citizens of Rome, so their lives looked and felt very different from the citizens of the empire. Nonetheless, Matthew supported the agenda of Rome by enforcing high taxation on his own countrymen, collecting information useful to Roman rule, and financing Jewish oppression from the oppressed. In this context, even though he was accepted by Jesus, Matthew was most likely despised and marginalized among the twelve.

Matthew was well connected with tax collectors and sinners according to his own writings in Matthew 9:9–10. Matthew brought a group of affluent, social outcasts to Jesus that no other disciple had in their network, with perhaps the exception of Judas. It was common for prostitutes, partiers, drunkards, and other "sinners" to run with the tax-collector crowd. Whatever loss of respect the tax collectors experienced from the Jews, their excessive wealth from Rome made up for it. Matthew lived a life the other disciples could not imagine or accept.

It's interesting to note that Jesus called Matthew as he sat at his tax collection station. This must have been somewhat of an awkward but powerful moment in the life of Matthew. Typical within the tax-collector trade, Matthew was meticulous with his details; he recorded the miracles, personal experiences, and teachings of Jesus.

Throughout Matthew's writings, he highlights Jesus's teachings on money and tax policies as recorded in Matthew 17:24; 22:21. Somehow Matthew must have felt vindicated when Jesus said "give to Caesar what belongs to Caesar, and give to God what belongs to God." Matthew could take comfort in knowing that the role of Caesar in Rome was not excluded from the philosophy of Jesus. Perhaps it made Matthew feel like there was a place for him in the kingdom of Jesus.

Judas Iscariot: Think special interest, D.C. lobbyist. Judas was the classic modern-day lobbyist or campaign director. His name means "celebrated one, the man." Judas was probably very good with people—a quick thinker and a networker. Judas moved seamlessly within the religious, non-religious, government, and business sectors. His modus operandi was usually posed or pointed to an obvious public concern. Somehow his concern led to personal gain and recognition (John 12:4–6).

It's interesting that Judas was the treasurer among the twelve. This demonstrates the power of his influence. Matthew, Philip, or Peter would seem to be better suited for counting money and distributing funds. The disciples reveal in their writings, after the fact, that Judas was an embezzler. Yet, during the time they were together, all the disciples perceived Judas as trustworthy and a partner with Christ. The disciples could not believe Judas would embezzle from their group finances. They perceived Judas to be a person of honor and integrity.

Judas' betrayal of Jesus and his suicide was an eye-opener to the disciples. They were shocked, dismayed, and disappointed that Judas actually betrayed Christ and took his own life. Judas sold Jesus for the same price one would pay for a sacrificial animal—thirty pieces of silver.

Although there was rampant disagreement among the twelve, Judas seemed to be the one disciple that the other eleven trusted and never suspected. Judas lived the unsuspected life. This provided him cover and gave him access to the places and the people of power like the chief priests, to whom Judas would deliver Jesus on the night of the betrayal. It also explains how the disciples could not recognize his motives until after his suicide.

When the disciples asked Jesus who would betray Him, Jesus said openly, "One of you who has just eaten from this bowl with me will betray me." At that moment, Judas was so bold to ask, "Rabbi, am I the one?" as he placed his hand in the same dish, signaling his identity as the betrayer (Matt. 26:23–25). Jesus's response was "You have said it." Yet none of the disciples, who were in the same room, watching and listening to this exchange, expected or accepted Judas as a betrayer.

In John 12, when Judas complained about Jesus being the recipient of an offering totaling an annual income, no one among the twelve challenged his conclusions or assumptions except Jesus. In fact, according to Matthew's account (Matt. 26:8), some agreed with Judas. Even after the events surrounding the death of Judas and the resurrection of Jesus, the disciples were still processing the actions of Judas.

It would be some 15 to 40 years later, as the Gospels were written that these older disciples would look back in time and refer to Judas as the betrayer of Jesus. Hindsight is always 20/20. Perhaps it was the lack of perception among the twelve that gave Judas opportunity to betray their Lord.

Judas would be the perfect betrayer—unseen, unnoticed, and unsuspected. By betraying Jesus, he would betray them all. Judas had equal opportunities to know Christ and commit to Him. But Judas had a distracted heart. Judas had no ability to sense the seasons and moments of Christ. He was blind to them because he had his own agenda. If Judas could not be at the center of Jesus's world, then Jesus would not be at the center of Judas's world.

AN AWKWARD QUESTION

Of all the questions asked in the New Testament, one of the most eye-opening occurs in Acts 1:6. Here the disciples asked, "Lord, has the time come for you to free Israel and restore our kingdom?" Jesus has died, risen from the dead, and is conveying an eternal kingdom on the disciples—and the disciples are still chasing political opportunities.

Jesus did not authorize an uprising, but rather a prayer meeting.

All of the disciples thought Jesus was going to restore the political power and kingdom to Israel. But they were wrong. His answer was not in changing an earthly political system, but in exchanging an earthly political system for a kingdom that cannot be shaken.

Jesus did not authorize an uprising, but rather a prayer meeting. His direction to them was simple: "You shall be my witnesses to the ends of the earth." Jesus did not supply them with power to rebel, but with the power to reveal that Jesus is the Son of God.

There is so much more to this story in the Book of Acts. But let me end this chapter with a few facts and thoughts. Perhaps the following thoughts will create a unifying understanding regarding the diversity of the disciples and the current political diversity among the body of Christ.

Fact #1. There was significant infighting, political misalignment, and positional indignation among the twelve disciples. Much of their disagreements centered around their political ideologies, agendas, and personal advancement. See Luke 9:46 and 22:24. These men experienced significant levels of dysfunction among themselves. They were often more distrusting than accepting of one another.

Even as Jesus began to finish His earthly ministry, He was still instructing and encouraging them to love one another. They were not a band of brothers at the Last Supper; they were a Band-Aid® of disciples. Jesus did not concern Himself with their dysfunction, only their motives and attitudes toward one another. John 15 makes this truth very clear. The commandment of Christ was to love one another. Political ideologies and agendas could not dilute the cross or the message of Jesus.

The signature of Jesus among the twelve was love, and the foundation was unity in believing Jesus was and is the Son of God. This was their litmus test. Anything less than the expressions of these attributes and the message of Jesus could be lost in the morass of history.

Fact #2. Not all of the disciples believed Jesus was the Messiah until after the resurrection. It seems highly improbable that the disciples doubted the divine attributes of Jesus, but it is very true. Reading through the Gospels provides incredible insight on the spiritual formation of the twelve. What is interesting is that each Gospel writer is careful not to tell a part of the story that is self-incriminating. Because Mark is not one of the twelve, he is very objective to record who said what. In fact, Mark is really the writer who tells the rest of the story about the disciple's spiritual development.

By Mark 4, Jesus has chosen the disciples. He had healed the paralytic and the blind man, cleansed the leper, healed Peter's mother-in-law, cast out many demons, healed the man with a crippled hand, healed the multitude, explained the unpardonable sin, and taught through the parables. The disciples had been with Jesus for an extended period of time, perhaps around twelve months or longer. They had seen Jesus work in the authority and power of God. He had explained some of the secret things of the kingdom to them. They had seen the God side of Jesus.

At the end of chapter 4, Jesus told the disciples to cross over the Sea of Galilee by boat. It was evening; Jesus was fatigued and fell asleep in the boat. During that time, a great storm arose and battered the boat in the waves. The boat was beginning to fill with water, and the disciples awakened Jesus and asked him a question. Their question bordered on the ridiculous: "Teacher, do you not care that we are perishing?" So Jesus arose, rebuked the winds and the waves, and immediately the surface of Galilee was calm. After Jesus rebuked them for their lack of faith, the disciples asked another seemingly ridiculous question amongst themselves: "Who can this be, that even the wind and the sea obey him?"

Jesus spoke openly to the disciples so they could understand that He was the Son of God. Jesus spent much of the first two-and-half years helping the disciples see He was truly God's Son. In Matthew 16:15–17, Jesus asks them plainly, "Who do you say I am?" Only one disciple, Peter, responds and claims Jesus is the Christ. The other eleven disciples are silent!

At the end of His time on earth, at the end of Last Supper, all of the disciples believed He was the Messiah (John 16:29–31). After that moment, they would all fall away and be restored to faith after the resurrection (Matt. 26:31; Luke 22:32). The last one to believe was Thomas in John 20:24–29.

This idea that all the disciples and followers believed on Jesus as God's Son immediately is a myth at worse and unfettered optimism at best. Until the end, they did not see Jesus as Savior. In Matthew 28:16, the disciples had gathered to the mountain Jesus appointed for them. Then verse 17 states, "When they saw him, they worshipped him—but some of them doubted!" For Jesus, the revealing of His Lordship was a continual effort after His resurrection until He ascended into heaven.

Fact #3. Even after the resurrection of Jesus, the disciples expected a new Israeli political kingdom. Their anticipation of a strong Jewish State free from Roman oppression never faded. It was the first question they asked Jesus as they were gathered together according to Acts 1:6.

Once Jesus ascended, they lived in the hope of His return. They had seen the oppression of their nation, and they understood the prophecies of a ruling Israel. They were passionate about this political reality because Jesus had told them they would judge the tribes of Israel (Matt. 19:28). This strong belief in Christ's immediate return may explain why the writers of the gospels and the specific books bearing their names were written twenty to thirty years after Christ's resurrection and ascension.

Like the Old Testament prophets, the disciples never saw the church age. They probably would not have organized the church on their own had it not been birthed at the feast of Pentecost. The disciples assumed the kingdom of God was a restored Israel. They were looking for a new nation, not a new spiritual organism.

Fact #4. The only common relationship among the disciples was Jesus. If Jesus had not selected these men, it's pretty obvious they would not have selected each other. In John 13:35, Jesus stated, "Your love for one another will prove to the world that you are my disciples." This was an actual statement, not an ideological tactic. Jesus made this statement because the disciples did not love one another.

Over and over again, Jesus would remind the disciples to love one another. After He washed their feet, He commanded them to wash the feet of one another. There are no recorded statements within the Scriptures or outside of the Scriptures that documents the disciples washing each others' feet.

In the absence of Jesus, the relationship among the disciples was selective, tense, and distant. Jesus taught the value of loving one another, not the ethics of liking one another. Jesus focused on their fellowship together and not on their friendship together.

In John 15:16, Jesus plainly tells them, "You didn't choose me. I chose you. I appointed you to go and produce lasting fruit." This statement was a pointed reminder that there was no consensus among them concerning Jesus. Jesus was the only one convinced of their need to be included as disciples.

Out of the twelve, Peter appears to be the primary influencer and leader of the disciples after Jesus. But, in reality, it appears he influenced less than half of the twelve. In John 21, Peter decides to go fishing and brings six others on the trip. Out of the six, only five were of the original disciples. More than half of the disciples were outside the social circle of Peter!

When Peter decided to have some "get away" time with friends, only five of the disciples were included. Although these twelve men had experienced Jesus together, they did not share a lot of experiences together in the absence of Jesus. They were spiritual brothers by spiritual birth, but not common friends.

THE POLITICAL OBSERVATIONS OF JESUS

After studying the four Gospels and the response of disciples and Jesus, there are five observations that can be attached to Jesus.

*1. Jesus selected the disciples knowing their
political leanings created tension and disputes*

among them (Matt. 10:1–4).

As difficult as it may be for you or me to imagine, Jesus was not politically motivated as it relates to earthly government. Throughout history, the church has always been anti-cultural to a large degree and therefore persecuted by a host of governments and political movements. Faith, and those who claim faith, has always been on a different side of the political spectrum.

The cross is not selective in who it saves, but it's thorough because it saves to the uttermost (Heb. 7:25).

Jesus selected the disciples because He was sending a message to those who would follow after Him. The message is that Jesus is bigger than political parties, ideologies, and philosophies. Jesus came to save people, not establish human governments. No matter a person's political doctrine or persuasion, there is room at the foot of the cross for everyone. The cross is not selective in who it saves, but it's thorough because it saves to the uttermost (Heb. 7:25).

2. Jesus tolerated political partisanship, but He would not tolerate a lack of faith or unbelief (Matt. 17:14–21).

Jesus was patient as His misguided disciples reasoned and debated politics. Occasionally, Jesus would rebuke the disciples or provide them with a teaching moment. However, for the most part, Jesus tolerated their political opining and bloviating. What Jesus would not put up with was their lack of faith.

Jesus viewed belief in God to be more critical than belief

in governments or rulers. There was no manual for voting God's way, but there was great demand for the disciples to function in faith and spiritual power. This segues into a valuable lesson. God does not care about our political victories as much as He cares about spiritual victories. Look at Luke 18:1–8.

> One day Jesus told his disciples a story to show that they should always pray and never give up. "There was a judge in a certain city," he said, "who neither feared God nor cared about people. A widow of that city came to him repeatedly, saying, 'Give me justice in this dispute with my enemy.' The judge ignored her for a while, but finally he said to himself, 'I don't fear God or care about people, but this woman is driving me crazy. I'm going to see that she gets justice, because she is wearing me out with her constant requests!'" Then the Lord said, "Learn a lesson from this unjust judge. Even he rendered a just decision in the end. So don't you think God will surely give justice to his chosen people who cry out to him day and night? Will he keep putting them off? I tell you, he will grant justice to them quickly! But when the Son of Man returns, how many will he find on the earth who have faith?"

Notice the issue in this passage was not political justice, although justice was needed. The real concern for Jesus was finding people on earth who would possess faith in the Son of God and not place their trust solely in the institutions of man. In these days before the return of the Lord, the church needs to make the message of the gospel and the ministry of the Holy Spirit its foremost priority. Political alliances can wait but the work of faith cannot. The world is starving for a faith-activated church!

*3. Jesus came to establish the infallible spiritual
kingdom, not a political kingdom (Matt. 6:33,
John 18:36).*

Over and over again, Jesus made it clear that His
kingdom was not of this world. When people wanted to
relegate His kingdom into a political voice, He pushed
back firmly and assertively (John 6:15; 18:36). One of the
major flaws of contemporary Christianity is a political
ideology that seeks to force the kingdom of God values on
non-kingdom individuals.

The apostle Peter came to recognize that we are a holy
nation of priests called out of darkness to proclaim Christ.
Our identification is in Christ as people who have obtained
mercy (1 Pet. 1:9–10). Christ-followers are sojourners and
pilgrims in this world, citizens of a heavenly realm, and
not primarily attached to failed political governmental
models on earth (1 Pet. 1:11).

When Christ-followers lose sight of this heavenly calling,
our efforts move to reclaiming worldly politics instead of
transforming human lives. Make no mistake; there is a
place for the believers' voice in politics. However, there is
no place for politics, candidates, or parties to substitute for
the purpose of the church. Humankind will never get government models right.

Jesus did not die to establish the best government on
the earth; He died to establish and empower His body on
the earth. Our focus must be bigger than politics and government; it must be kingdom focused, front and center.
Anything else is a distraction, not a destiny.

*4. The primary core value in the politics of Jesus is
love for one another, not tolerance. Love creates
tolerance, but tolerance doesn't create love (John
13:34–35).*

The true litmus test of kingdom behavior is loving one another (John 15:12). Jesus told the disciples that essentially they were being watched by the world. The only distinguishing mark that would be noticed by others was their love for one another (John 13:34–35). Love would baffle the world. *Love does not produce tolerance; love produces patience.*

Christ followers must cease the attacks on one another in the name of Jesus. Christ-followers can disagree without being disagreeable. A believer can point to differences based upon wisdom and understanding without disparaging one another in the media and in social media. If there is a scriptural principle that needs to be embedded into political discourse or dislodged from a conversation, then have a robust, sane, and respectful conversation.

The Constitution and Bill of Rights empower America's citizenry recourse to political decisions, actions, or ideologies that conflict with their faith. However, there is a biblical way to present a counter argument or political side without becoming belligerent, obnoxious, or disdaining. The biggest philosophical move of the far left is to claim tolerance as the acceptable response to their ideologies or actions, while exercising intolerance toward those who oppose them.

This argument of tolerance is a ploy; it's a faux principle that works in the hand of the user and not the recipient. Consider this...when Christ-followers practice tolerance, they are abandoning the principle of God's love and disempowering their faith. Tolerance will never produce love. But when Christ-followers respond with love, they become empowered to be patient and speak truth. Love is the primary principle of God's kingdom.

5. The body of Christ is unified through Christ, not politics, ideologies, or philosophies (1 Cor. 12:12–18).

When Christ-followers lead with their political stance first, the body of Christ is divided. In 1 Corinthians 1:13, Paul asked the Corinthians a question that needs to be asked now: "Has Christ been divided into factions?" Politics has become personal in a way the founding fathers never intended. Believers must learn that our confession of "Jesus Christ is Lord" triumphs over all political ideologies and philosophies. Our identity is in Jesus Christ, not our political registration. Churches are beginning to choose political stances and positions, and embed their faith around their political disposition. Pastors are making it clear where they stand and encouraging their congregation to accept political positions and tolerances. The flock of Jesus is being forced to choose shepherds and congregations based upon political ideology instead of scriptural understanding and doctrines. Church is evolving into a body of people who belong and fellowship together based upon political ideology, instead of a blood washing through Jesus Christ.

America needs pastors and spiritual voices who will communicate the Bible, free from political inferences, biases, or ideals. Spiritual leaders can no longer dilute the Word of God with a political philosophy of tolerance, seeking the applause of special interest groups, the media, or the culture. Christianity was founded on the cross, and it is best lived out in the culture where it stands for righteousness, salvation, and freedom from sin. This idea of being a politically correct church is dividing the body of Christ, confusing the saints, and diffusing the faith.

The one who unites the church is Jesus Christ. Our unity flows from abiding in the Word and seeking the unity of the Spirit. Until the church returns to its foundation, its voice will lack power, and its influence will be disregarded. If we do not unite in the name of Jesus, we will not unite at all.

CONSIDER THIS

As believers, we are to accept and love everyone, whether we agree politically or not. We are to overcome challenges, disagreements, and issues through wisdom, grace, and truth. We are united through Christ; partisan politics is a dividing distraction that the body of Christ should avoid. Don't play into the hands of those who leverage division.

Leading people into the Lordship of Jesus means looking beyond their political leanings, lifestyles, preferences, and ideologies. We are one church, confessing one Lord Jesus Christ and glorifying one God as one body! Let's operate as one body, making room for differences of opinion while holding unswervingly to the truths found in God's Word. The vast differences dividing the American Church are built on social or cultural issues which either conflict with Scripture or have no scriptural directives. When believers choose political preferences instead of scriptural authority, the church is compromised and the culture is lost.

In Christ, there is no Democrat, Republican, or Independent (1 Cor. 12:13–14). We are either saved or unsaved, forgiven or unforgiven, righteous or unrighteous. We are one in Christ as we serve one another, preferring those who are weak or immature in the faith.

Jesus demonstrated through His own selection of disciples that a variety of political philosophies, ideologies, and governmental principles could all come to the same conclusion—that Jesus Christ is Lord. Jesus did not come to fix the world; He came to save us from our sin. His purpose was to seek and save that which was lost.

The gospel is not about voting; it's about victory. It's not about seeking the same government; it's about seeking the same God. As we gather into political cycles and political circles, let us remember the driving principle of Jesus, "But seek first the kingdom of God and His righteousness, and all these things shall be added to you" (Matt. 6:33, NKJV).

HAVE YOU MET JESUS?

Before this chapter ends, the real question is not about your political affiliation, but about your spiritual identity. *Do you know Jesus as your Lord and Savior?* That's an easy question to answer because it's either yes or no. If your answer is "Yes! I know Jesus as my Lord and Savior," then we rejoice with you. But if you cannot honestly answer that question with a yes, the next few paragraphs are for you.

You see, God loves you so much He could not bear being eternally separated from you. Our wrongs against God are sins, and sin separates us from God. So Jesus Christ left heaven and came to the earth in human form. He became subject to human weakness, need, and temptation. You see, Jesus put Himself to the test wearing humanity in all its weakness but He remained strong because of His God nature. Jesus Christ did not sin on earth; He lived a sinless life. Jesus lived in righteousness and holiness so He could offer Himself as a sacrifice for us by dying on the cross for our sins. Because Jesus was sinless, death had no affect on Him. Jesus rose from the dead and ascended to heaven, where He reigns and rules over all things.

You can experience forgiveness of sin and receive God's peace, hope, and love by praying this prayer: "Dear Jesus, I believe You came to earth, lived as a human, and died for my sin. I believe You rose from the dead and ascended into heaven. So I confess my sins and ask to you to forgive me. By faith, I receive your forgiveness, and I confess "Jesus Christ is Lord!" Amen!

If you prayed that prayer, the Bible declares in Romans 10:9–10 that you are eternally saved! Begin to thank Jesus for His righteousness to be activated in your life. Begin reading the Bible, preferably the Books of Mark, John, and Ephesians first. Find a great church near you and begin to attend. Get ready for Jesus to take you into greater and better things! And...drop me an email at pastor@genesis-people.com and share with me what God has done in your life! God bless you!

Chapter 4

SAMARIA IS CALLING

The laden phrase "identity politics" has come to signify a wide range of political activity and theorizing founded in the shared experiences of injustice of members of certain social groups.[1]

Identity politics is a political style that focuses on the issues relevant to various groups defined by a wide variety of shared characteristics, including, but not limited to, race, social class, religion, sex, gender, ethnicity, ideology, nationality, sexual orientation, gender expression, culture, currency, shared history, medical conditions, profession, and other of the many ways in which people differ from each other, and into which they may be classified or classify themselves.[2]

A STUNNING TRANSFORMATION HAS occurred in America in the last decade. We have become a divided nation, focused on differences instead of similarities. We have become an offended citizenship. It seems as if almost every race, ethnic group, culture, religion, gender, and orientation has some offense against the others. Colleges and universities are watching students protest over micro-aggressions. Did you get that? They are protesting over small, petty disagreements they now term as micro-aggressions! As a nation, we have lost sight of our similarities and developed our insecurities from our differences.

We are no longer Americans; we are labeled and hyphenated Americans. Our differences are pushed forward and projected as a badge of intimidating sensitivities. The new equation of social justice is based on how great the offense is, plus the severity of the historical or empirical wound, which equals the final outcome of justice and fairness. And yes…it's about both justice and fairness. Justice, being the legal standard inclusive of penalties and damages—and fairness, being the social standard inclusive of shaming and personal destruction.

It seems as if there is a culture contest to become the most wounded, offended, and oppressed people group in America. People think with their feelings; objectivity is out, and subjectivity is everything. Rights have become conditional, success has become marginal, and unity has become fictional. It's as if we are working to become obtuse thinkers, who are philosophically deep and fundamentally ignorant.

Our arrogance has led to pettiness. We have overcomplained and underperformed. We have replaced the spirit of agreement with our differences and indifferences. Our wounds must be ratified, justified, and compensated. We have lost the moral equivalent of gratitude and graciousness. The end result is violence has become more violent, and the sarcastic vitriol against sanity has intimidated many people from voicing their intelligent discontent. As free speech fades, fascism rises.

The pressure from media scrutiny is threatening and real. One inappropriate social media post and a person's life is imbued with the permanency of its own failure. There is no tolerance, just anger. There is no forgiveness, just hatred. There are no sensibilities, just irrationality.

America is experiencing cultural and social vertigo. Society has lost its balance and consciousness from the blunt-force trauma of racial separatism, identity politics, and victimization that fills the courts, cable channels, and media continuously. Foundations of trust have been eroded in an atmosphere of pain, offense and distrust. There is very little left in our culture that is dependable, stable, and predictable.

There is a societal fraud being exercised against our citizenry. We are told we must accept these ideological and philosophical changes as the new normal. Political correctness has given birth to identity politics. Economic division is the reason for disparity. Hatred is targeted toward those who have more. There is a philosophical shift pushing Americans away from rugged individualism towards fragile collectivism.

Symbolism has replaced substance. People make expedient judgments and decisions based on assumption or perception. Dr. Martin Luther King would shame all of us for not building the necessary societal character that bestows dignity, respect, and honor to all people in spite of their human condition.

There is also a societal feud being waged against the economic classes in America. There is an economic ideology that believes that whatever someone else possesses is a barrier for others to possess something similar. It's literally a mentality of having one pie for desert and needing to equalize the portions. Would it not make more sense to bake another pie?

There is an attack against sound thought and sound thought processes. Standardizing curricula, entrance exams, and other means of evaluation are producing a lesser-educated citizenry functioning at the lowest, common level. Individual thoughts and ideas are dangerous if they challenge the collective conclusions or conventional wisdom. We are in a rapid race to the bottom of democracy, liberty, and constitutional freedoms. This descent is creating a negative momentum that brings with it the ineptness and irresponsibility of blame-focused policies, identity politics, and continual social wounds.

> The body of Christ is anointed and called to release grace across the land, not remove or obstruct it.

In America, the issues associated with identity politics are demanding a societal response. As believers, it's very dangerous to wade into the pool of human offense. It's almost impossible to maintain faith and fellowship when the natural core of identity politics is separation and conflagration. It is a slippery slope that is unstable, unpredictable, and unhealthy. Fairness cannot speak to injustice any more than anger can speak to hope. The body of Christ is anointed and called to release grace across the land, not remove or obstruct it. When Christ-followers enter the fray of politicizing offense, the vessels of healing are hindered.

As Christ-followers, our voice needs to be heard, but it cannot be heard through the corridors of the common channels promoting offense and disparity. Our voice needs to be felt, but it cannot be attached to the emotive forces of anger, disgust, and revenge. Our voice needs to be different than the humanistic philosophies that have created identity politics. This is our country, and this is our moment to declare justice without impudence and healing without judgment. It is time for the body of Christ to rise above the political quagmire and present the full picture of Christ as a healer and restorer of the nations.

THE JOURNEY INTO 500 YEARS

Something interesting happened on the way to Galilee. The Bible states in John 4:4, "But Jesus needed to go through Samaria." Samaria was the last place a good Jew would travel through. There was a better, alternate route to Galilee that bypassed Samaria; it was the route most traveled, even though it was longer and more time consuming. But Jesus needed to go Samaria. The word *need* in this verse means to be literally bound and tied, drawn and compelled. Something on the inside of Jesus was redirecting His route; He had to pass through Samaria. Samaria was calling.

Samaria was like the rougher side of town. It was where "those people" lived. Samaritans were looked down on by the Jews; they were considered a lesser race. Samaritans were the social outcasts of the Jews. According to Jewish social traditions, a dog belonging to a Jewish family had higher social standing than a woman of Samaria. Samaritans were like the neighbor you wish would move off your street, or like the guy in the office you hope will get fired; these people were the regional scourge.

The grudge between the Samaritans and the Jews was more than five hundred years old. The historical tension began 725 years earlier. Yes, you read that correctly. For over five hundred years, there was hatred, disdain, and prejudice between these two ethnic groups. The wounds of their identity politics ran deep, and the blood was still fresh. Hatred and wounds were passed from generation to generation on both sides. Nothing changed until Jesus went through Samaria.

Margaret Mowczko explains the historical tension between these two ethnic groups with a simple accuracy.

> All the kings of Israel, without exception, were unfaithful and disobedient to God. They embraced

idolatrous religions and were extremely wicked. After repeated prophetic warnings about coming disaster—unless Israel repented—the northern kingdom of Israel was overpowered by the Assyrians in around 724 BC.

Most of the Israeli inhabitants—those who survived the attack—were taken to foreign lands where they were assimilated into the native populations (2 Kings 17.5–6; 17:22–41). These northern tribes are referred to as the "lost tribes of Israel." However, a few groups of Israelite families retained their ancestral integrity.

The Assyrians sent five eastern tribes to live in Northern Israel. These five tribes brought with them their own foreign religions and customs. The tribes were sent with the purpose of diminishing the Israeli identity and culture. The eastern foreigners intermarried with the remaining, much-depleted Israeli population. This hybrid people group was the beginning of the Samaritans.

In 586 BC, the southern kingdom of Judah was also conquered by the Babylonians (2 Chron. 36:15ff), and the whole of Israel and Judah came to be known as Samaria. Many Jews were exiled from their homeland and taken captive into Babylon for 70 years, as prophesied by Jeremiah (Jer. 25:11–12; 2 Chron. 36:21). The Jewish population was taken in several stages to Babylon. It seems that only the poorest, sickest, and least skilled were ultimately left behind. These remaining people intermarried with their northern neighbors with the result that foreign beliefs and customs mixed with Jewish beliefs and customs.

The Jews were mostly treated well in Babylon. While some Jews lamented their captivity in a foreign land (e.g. Psalm 137), others became established in their new communities. When the Persian King Cyrus was divinely led to allow the Jews to return

70 years later (Ezra 1:1ff), only the most devout Jews returned to Jerusalem, with the purpose of rebuilding the city and its Temple.

The Babylonian exile had been a punishment for Judah's unfaithfulness to God, and the Jews had learned from it. The returned Jews were zealous for God and righteous living, and, for the most part, they never again engaged in blatant idolatry. The returning Jews were keen to rebuild the Jerusalem Temple so that they could worship God in the way he had prescribed. The Samaritans offered to help the Jews in rebuilding the Temple, but this offer was scornfully rejected (Ezra 4:1–5).[3]

So fast forward to Ezra 5, and here is where the wounds get worse. The "pure blooded Jews" rejected the offers of help from the "lowly" Samaritans to rebuild the Temple. These Jews were prejudiced and felt the Samaritans were unworthy of this honor.

The response of the Jews was a huge insult to the Samaritans. The Samaritans were angered and sent a letter to the King of Persia. The letter basically said:

1. *The Jews are planning to rebel against you after you help rebuild their city.*

2. *Once they complete building what you are financing, they will stop paying taxes to your kingdom.*

3. *Do your homework, and you'll see their intention is to create their own dominion and break free from your rule.*

The letter was effective. Once the King of Persia read it, he ordered that the building of the Temple be halted immediately. It remained unfinished until a new king was crowned over Persia. The Jews never forgot this political attack from the Samaritans.

> Meanwhile, the Samaritans had developed their own compromised version of Judaism. The Samaritans still believed in the God of the Jews, but they worshiped at Mount Gerizim (instead of Jerusalem) with their own, adapted, worship practices. The Samaritans also had their own Pentateuch in Aramaic, which differed from the Hebrew Pentateuch in places. To this day, the Samaritans do not accept the poetic and prophetic books of the Hebrew Scriptures.
>
> In around 400 BC the Samaritans built a temple on Mount Gerizim. This caused a lot of tension and hostility between the Jews and the Samaritans. The Jews ultimately destroyed the Samaritan temple in 128/9 BC. Nevertheless, the Samaritan religious community still survives today. Most Jews regarded the Samaritans as ignorant, superstitious, mongrels, outside of God's favor or consideration.[4]

When Jesus showed up almost 150 years later (after the destruction of the Samaritan temple), the Samaritans were practicing "identity politics." They had a cultural wound against another ethnic group over an injustice that began five hundred years earlier. The retaliation of the Jews against the Samaritans was excessive. The Samaritans delayed the building of a Jewish worship temple, but the Jews destroyed the Samaritans' worship temple.

The Jews had their temple construction financed by the King of Persia, whereas the Samaritans had to pay for their own temple. The Samaritans were economically disadvantaged, and their ethnicity had endured an unjust ethnic cleansing. While the Jews had been in exile, they had not been exterminated. The tension between these two ethnicities was absolutely incredible.

Adding insult to injury, the Jews further impacted Samaria's economy by boycotting travel through their territory. The Jews traveled a longer route going to northern Galilee from southern Judea, instead of bringing finances and trade into Samaria through a shorter, more direct route. It was an unnecessary, ruthless tension.

Only 50 kilometers separated the two capital cities of Samaria and Jerusalem. But these two people groups were hundreds of years apart in matters of race, economic prosperity, and social justice. This tension was nothing but wounds, insults, and injustice all wrapped into a neat, religious box that looked acceptable from one side and felt deplorable to the other side. This was the identity politics environment Jesus needed to enter.

NO PERFECT TIME

Jesus sensed a driving need to take the journey through Samaria. He was anointed for that moment and situation as He followed the inner, intuitive voice of the Holy Spirit. An entire village was changed because Jesus showed up and spoke life into their wounds.

As Christ-followers, we are going to have to journey into our culture's Samaria. We have to begin speaking the commonsense voice of Jesus into issues that have carried grief, pain, bitterness, and separation for decades and generations. We must embrace the desolate regions of the human spirit and be present to understand historical injustice while pointing people to hope and healing. This is not easy; Samaria is a den of lions for the virtuous. But Samaria is calling, and its injustice is compelling. People are allowing past wounds to define their future potential. This is becoming a reciprocal generational curse that must be cancelled with compassion and truth.

The absence of the body of Christ in these political

identity issues and conversations has given a platform for humanistic, ungodly solutions that have perpetuated frustration, unrest, and vehemence. It's a great time for the church to enter into community dialogue and bring the presence of peace, understanding, and wisdom. The only way to change the conversation and influence the results is to enter into the issues and conversations.

There is no perfect time to enter Samaria. For the Samaritans, the perfect time was five hundred years earlier. Jesus wasn't on the earth then, but when He did come to the earth He went to Samaria. There are times you have to clean the kitchen when you did not make the mess, because the meal you're making now can't wait for the previous mess-maker to show up. We are losing generations of Americans because someone or some group was historically irresponsible. It's as if we are waiting for the offended side to forget about their issue and move on, or for the offender to return from the dead and fix things. Maybe the reason we as Christ-followers possess the earth at this time is because we are called and anointed to enter Samaria and bring healing, restoration, and reconciliation.

It is worth mentioning that not all offenses are legitimate injustices. Just because someone is offended does not mean an actual offense has occurred. Offenses are sometimes the result of immaturity, oversensitivity, or excessive reaction. Sometimes offenses are the result of positive change and growth. The wise seek a process similar to the approach of Jesus. If there truly is an offense or injustice, Jesus gives a process to reconstruct legitimate communication and facilitate recovery and healing.

THE PAIN OF SYCHAR

In John 4:4, Jesus arrives in a city named Sychar. Sychar means to be intoxicated, literally drunken, and it comes from a root word that means tipsy, to be in a state of stupor. Self-medication through alcohol, drugs, or other forms of escapism behaviors is often a common destination for people who are offended, wounded, bitter, or feel betrayed by justice. It's no accident Jesus came to this city, and it's no coincidence this city is called Sychar.

As in most Middle-Eastern cultures, a name defined one's nature, actions, experience, or future. After hundreds of years of passing the offense forward, hope evaporated in the heat of hurt and rage. From that moment on, anger from injustice numbed the human soul. Alcohol or chemical relief was sought as a coping mechanism. Dysfunction, dependency, and moral apathy thrived in a place like Sychar.

It was here in Sychar that Jesus met a woman drawing water at the noon hour. Her presence at the well during this time of the day was an indicator of her social standing and lack of acceptance. She wasn't at the well in the midday heat because of a hangover, she was there because she was not welcomed at the well in the cool of the morning.

In Eastern cultures, the women came to the public wells in the morning or evening, not in heat of the day. But for women who have been shunned or shamed, their draw time was at noon. Midday was when the disrespected women had access to the well.

Jesus was thirsty. His disciples were looking for a place to purchase food, and they were not near the well. As this woman came to draw water, Jesus asked her for a drink. His request floored her. She was amazed a Jewish man would speak to her, a Samaritan woman, especially at that time of day. Jews didn't speak to Samaritans; that's just the way it was. Jews certainly did not drink after Samaritans, especially a woman.

When Jesus requested a simple drink of water, an entire conversation broke out that dealt with past offenses and cultural wounds. It culminated in life change for this woman and her city. It was the reason why Jesus needed to go through Samaria.

Take a moment and read the account in John 4:3–45. It was from this passage that the identity politics conversation of Jesus was outlined. Jesus gave us a process to follow as we hold these difficult conversations. Not all conversations may get finished in one afternoon or in a few days. However, there was a clear process Jesus followed.

It could be that after you've read, reflected, and reviewed this process, you'll find some additional values that can be added to or mingled into the following statements.

THE SAMARIA PROCESS OF JESUS

When you're sitting down at the table of issues, wounds, and injustice...

1. Open the conversation with a non-defensive subject; ask for their help.
   Asking someone for help is the quickest way to build a relationship (John 4:7–8).

2. Respond with answers that create curiosity.
   Curiosity pulls people deeper into conversations (John 4:10).

3. Talk hope instead of history.
   Let people know the question(s) you're ready to positively answer (John 4:10).

4. Intently listen; then respectfully respond.
   Answer the most meaningful question first (John 4:11–14).

5. Address pertinent issues within their culture.
   Begin with the truth; search until you find something true (John 4:15–18).

6. Avoid meaningless controversies, especially about the past.
   Speak confidently of life-changing solutions through God! (John 4:19–22).

7. Answer clearly; avoid complicated responses.
   Short, clear answers are best when issues are deep or complicated (John 4:23–24).

8. Welcome their thoughts, understandings, and revelations.
   Whenever possible, build the conversation on their statements (John 4:25).

9. Highlight the closest, most effective solution(s).
   Be direct, concise, and accurate (John 4:26).

10. Encourage people to process solutions away from the table. They need opportunities to share their experiences and questions with their core relationships.
    People are most confident in decisions that are shared and affirmed (John 4:27–30).

11. Continually point people to the bigger picture/vision.
    Avoid petty stuff, even from close relationships (John 4:32–38).

12. Welcome others into the conversation; develop mutual relationships.
    It's a healthy sign when others want to enter into the process (John 4:39–42).

13. Understand your part in the process.
    Empower others to complete what has begun; finish your purpose and move on.

Stay only as long as your strengths or gifts are required (John 4:43–45).

14. Point people to Jesus.
Jesus is the answer to every human condition (John 14:6).

THE IDENTITY OF JESUS

The American Church is leading itself into an identity crisis. Over the past ten years, the onslaught of the media, special interest, and other agenda-oriented groups has worked to silence the voice of Christianity in America. Atheists groups, humanistic groups, the ACLU, the Southern Poverty Law Center, and other organizations have waged an all-out attack on Christian rights, values, and legal permissions. They have identified the most conservative, Christian groups and relabeled them as hate groups. The attack is centered only on the name of Jesus; other faiths like Islam have been given a free pass.

The freedom of religion is being whittled away to freedom from religion. Gay couples are suing Christians who own bakeries, forcing them to bake a wedding cake for a gay wedding or go out of business. That same gay couple, however, will not sue a Muslim bakery or a Jewish bakery—only the Christians. Christian holidays like Good Friday, Easter, Christmas, and other special days are under attack in the courts. This is all part of the attack against a believer's identity in Christ. Even monuments that honor the dead with a symbolic cross are being legally challenged in court; often those cases are won, forcing the symbol of the cross away from public view.

These are not just Christian values or symbolic icons; these matters coalesce around our spiritual identity. Christians have accepted losing to the point we have quit fighting. Occasionally, there is a win in our column, and we hold onto hope a little longer, only to lose all confidence at the next big loss.

Satan has always attacked believers in the area of their spiritual identity in Christ. This is his pattern; he began this strategy with Jesus. In Matthew 4:3, the tempter came to Jesus after completing a forty-day fast. No doubt Jesus was spiritually full and physically empty. The very first words out of the mouth of the devil came in the form of a question, challenging the identity of Jesus. Twice the questions began, "If you are the Son of God..." This was a direct attack on the identity of Jesus.

The devil understands that if we become insecure about our identity, we will become ineffective in our faith. If we are constantly wondering if we are truly saved from the judgment of hell, we will lack boldness and be full of self-condemnation. It's really important we clarify and understand our identity in Jesus Christ.

As this chapter concludes, the following statements are strategically written to remind and empower Christ-followers. You are encouraged to search through these scriptures and adopt these identity statements or develop statements of your own.

My identity is in Christ because:

1. He is my life and the light of my salvation (John 1:4).

2. He has overcome the darkness (John 1:5).

3. He gave me the right to become a child of God (John 1:12).

4. He is the Word who became flesh, full of grace and truth (John 1:14).

5. He has given me eternal life (John 5:24).

6. He has authority to execute justice (John 5:27).

7. He is the resurrection and the life (John 11:25).

8. He is the way, the truth, and the life (John 14:6).

9. He has opened the way for me to fellowship with the Holy Spirit (John 16:7).

10. He has given me authority to do greater things (John 14:12).

11. He has given me the glory of the Father (John 17:22).

When you focus on who you are, you forget what has hurt you or who has wounded you. As Christ-followers, our identity is not in wounds and offenses of the past. Our identity is in our healer and forgiver who is present and working in our lives. Siding with an offense continuously never brings healing; it only promotes bitterness.

Our politically incorrect Jesus is the one who can mend the soul of humanity and the fabric of our culture.

Life is not fair, but God is faithful. Promoting your wound for justice and identifying with your pain for leverage is the strategy of the evil one. Jesus called us to forgive and release the offense, the wound, and the pain. Your identity is either in your pain or in your Savior; you cannot have it both ways.

There will be no healing across the identity wounds of this

country until the church stands up and proclaims healing through Jesus Christ. Our politically incorrect Jesus is the one who can mend the soul of humanity and the fabric of our culture. Injustice has no standing in the court of Christ. We as Christ-followers are either leading people into an identity with Christ or denying such an identity exists.

I have often wondered what the real effect was on the woman with whom Jesus spoke at the well. It's somewhat obvious that after five marriages and one live-in affair, she was broken on the inside. When I read this passage, there is always a flurry of unanswered questions.

- Did she marry the man she was living with?

- Did she break off that immoral relationship?

- When she accepted Jesus as Messiah, how was she fixed on the inside?

- What did her life become?

- Was she ever welcomed at the well in the cool of the day?

Scripture does not address these questions directly. What it does say is that her life changed so rapidly and significantly, other people became open to the same message she received. Once she received the refreshing water of salvation, she experienced completeness. Jesus bestowed on her dignity and respect. He gave her in a moment what had been missing for a lifetime.

It always amazes me how Jesus pursues the broken, the outcast, the wounded, and the hopeless. Her life looked a lot like other broken lives in Sychar; it was just that her life had become more public. It's been said we make our choices, and then our choices make us. Isn't it comforting to know Christ has made a different choice? His choice was to redeem our wrong, hurtful, and foolish choices to bring life, hope and transformation to those of us living in Sychar and in Samaria.

I believe the reason Scripture does not answer my litany of questions is because I don't really need those answers to live in Christ. I believe this woman experienced an inner healing when her Messiah hunted her down for a cold drink of water and an explosive conversation on a hot Samaritan day. I believe this woman had a change in her identity. She moved from being wounded to being whole, from brokenness to completeness, from living in pain to living in promise. She will always remember the day Jesus came to Sychar, the day Jesus came for her.

If there has ever been a message every church can proclaim, it is this message: "This is how much God loved the world: He gave his Son, his one and only Son. And this is why: so that no one need be destroyed; by believing in Him, anyone can have a whole and lasting life. God didn't go to all the trouble of sending his Son merely to point an accusing finger, telling the world how bad it was. He came to help, to put the world right again" (John 3:16–17, THE MESSAGE). This is the message of a new identity—a message that not only changes the identity of those living in Sychar, but the identity of those living in America.

Chapter 5

THE PERFECT IMMIGRANT

JESUS HAD A way of speaking words with conviction, insight, and wisdom. He possessed an ability to convince and agitate simultaneously. He was a theological artisan, who laced dynamic, eternal principles into simple life parables. He could baffle the attorney and professional scribe with an ordinary question. Jesus spoke with redolent ease, connecting seamlessly with the most simpleminded and brokenhearted.

Jesus also spoke key words, phrases, and sentences that encompassed human nature. He called the woman with a flow of blood for twelve years, "Daughter" (Mark 5:34). This woman was considered ceremonially unclean because of her continuous menstruation flow. She could not worship at the women's court in the Temple or enter into marriage covenant because of her condition. She lived in a perpetual state of religious uncleanliness and aloneness. Most likely, her life had been void of support and acceptance, so Jesus spoke to her what she needed to hear most. He healed her body and then revived her soul with the simple word "Daughter."

Just a few moments later, Jesus engaged the inner fear of grief-stricken parents with the simple phrase, "Do not be afraid; only believe" (Mark 5:36, NKJV). Walking into a home filled with mourners, Jesus did not allow reality to overcome destiny. He simply closed off the room and commanded this young girl to rise up. His words were so few and so powerful; His voice redirected life on earth and eternity.

After studying and researching the voice of Jesus in the Jewish culture, I began to wonder if the voice and words of Jesus spoke into the contentious complexities of the current political culture in America. Surely the environment of Roman oppression paralleled some of the extreme issues of our free society at least once or twice. There had to be the something in the voice of Jesus then that reaches forward now into this new millennium.

Jesus was a theological artisan, who laced dynamic, eternal principles into simple life parables.

Jesus, knowing the end from the beginning, could not come to earth to save humankind and avoid speaking to the issues that could destroy humankind. After researching His voice, His actions, and experiences, it became obvious to me that Jesus had thoughtfully spoken into these issues. However, clearly hearing His words over the cultural noise of these issues would require silencing current political ideologies. It would necessitate both a depth of maturity and understanding. His answers demanded laying down comfortable assumptions and dealing with uncomfortable issues and answers.

The apex of these issues began with understanding the very origin of the Savior on earth. Was Jesus only the God-incarnate Savior who came to earth from heaven, or was Jesus the God-incarnate Savior who emigrated from heaven to earth and then immigrated across cultures or nations while on the earth? Could the appearance and history of Jesus bring understanding to the current

immigration issues facing America? It's amazing how
Jesus and the Bible address the issue known in America
as immigration.

THE REAL TENSION OF IMMIGRATION

This subject of immigration contains a lot of emotion and
a lot of politics. Over the last few years, America has seen
its own laws and policies set aside and ignored due to the
flow of immigration. Honestly, people on all sides of this
issue are frustrated, struggling, or angry with the political
manipulation and legislative apathy surrounding this issue.

In the absence of political clarity, a vague cloud of political correctness has emerged. What frustrates many is the
absence of a reasonable plan to return illegal immigrants
to their homeland, establish responsible residency for them
in the USA, or give them a path to legal status and perhaps
citizenship. This continuous platform of indecision has
reduced immigrants to political pawns of special interests.

Their legitimate needs and issues are being concealed.
The legitimate needs and issues associated with their presence in this country are being underreported and misconstrued. One side sees them as potential cheap labor while
another side sees them as potential votes; very few politicians see them as people.

When searching for what is the right faith response to
this issue, sooner or later the discussion has to involve
this historical truth: Jesus would be considered an immigrant. After all, He did emigrate from heaven to earth,
and the accommodations were somewhat cramped until
His arrival! More than that, the family of Jesus emigrated
from Bethlehem to Egypt to save the young Child's life.

Look at Matthew 2:13–15:

> After the wise men were gone, an angel of the Lord
> appeared to Joseph in a dream. "Get up! Flee to
> Egypt with the child and his mother," the angel said.
> "Stay there until I tell you to return, because Herod is
> going to search for the child to kill him." That night
> Joseph left for Egypt with the child and Mary, his
> mother, and they stayed there until Herod's death.
> This fulfilled what the Lord had spoken through the
> prophet: "I called my Son out of Egypt."

These verses tucked away in Matthew lead us to make one accurate conclusion. The conclusion is that if Jesus had not been able to immigrate to Egypt, there would be no Jesus. He would have been slaughtered in an infanticide carried out by King Herod.

Americans are currently being torn apart from two competing principles. The first principle involves embracing the legal process of the law; the second principle involves embracing compassion for the human condition. There has been a "strategic placement" of situational ethics embedded into this polarizing argument where compassion and fairness must collide on the altar of justice and legal process.

The liberal persuasion of America seeks to transform the future voting base of the citizenry by establishing a permanent underclass. Bringing people into this country who are dependent on the government for food, housing, funds, and survival creates an underclass of dependency that justifies big government and garners Democrat votes. Those who promote socialistic ideas where opportunities become rights have become the face of hope to this underclass. It's not necessary for these people to learn English, get jobs, or become educated. Their existence validates active compassion for the unfortunate human condition. There are few solutions given or provided for these people, other than government solutions. Americans are seeing through this intention and are against dependency for the sake of compassion. Compassion empowers; it does not produce greater dependency.

The conservative persuasion of America seeks to protect the future voting base of the citizenry by removing soft border policies and creating more orderly immigration processes. They believe legal citizenship is an orderly process that educates and qualifies foreign immigrants to understand, value, and protect America's democracy and its Constitution. Their approach is beholden to the Constitution, the Bill of Rights, and the Federalists Papers. Conservatives typically believe the higher principle of long-term benefit to the country is order first, and then compassion.

Tucked in between the conservatives and progressives are liberal-leaning Republicans who do not care so much about political power, court appointments, and political appointees as they do about creating wealth. These bureaucrats see illegal immigrants as cheap labor that can be treated poorly for the sake of profit. They have already assumed that immigrants will vote for big government and their political party will lose in future elections. The best political insurance these bureaucrats can get is excessive wealth from ambitious business practices. They are not looking for votes or constitutional values; they are searching for money and wealth creation. The tension regarding immigration is significant. Much more is at stake than border policies and immigration processes.

Some questions beg to be asked, such as what would Jesus do or say regarding the issues of immigration? How would He direct His church, His body, to respond in this political climate? What is the right, biblical response to this growing challenge of illegal immigration?

There are basically five tensions that fuel the debate regarding immigration. They are:

1. Foreign culture versus constitutional culture.

2. Ethnic identity versus American citizenry.

3. System dependency versus self-productivity.

4. Lesser elements versus contributors.

5. Permanent legal status versus citizenship.

Let's look at each tension briefly.

1. Foreign culture versus constitutional culture

This is a tension between life cultures. When people immigrate into the United States, they are expected to set aside their foreign ideas of government and abide by the Constitution. What is happening in America is the fruition of a progressive constitutional mentality that abandons governing principles for governing ethics. The difference is that principles are based on absolutes while ethics are based on behavior.

The diluting of the constitutional culture for that of foreign interpretation and understanding erases the primary foundation of America. The Constitution and the Bill of Rights are unique to America and the only safeguards American citizens have against government overreach. Unrestrained immigration has the ability to dilute the unique restraints of our government and the unique privileges of our citizenry.

2. Ethnic identity versus American citizenry

America is made up of many diverse ethnic and religious groups. Up until this century, there was a built-in respect for these differences with an expectation for majority similarities. However, with the open door of unbridled immigration, people are coming into America and holding onto their own cultures while resistant toward transitioning into the fabric of American citizenry. The gap between ethnic identity and American similarities is growing wider with each passing day.

Immigrants are keeping their native language and not learning English as their primary language. Demands from special interest groups are being placed on businesses, schools, and the government to adapt to the limitations of immigrants. Bilingual signage is now common in stores, banks, and public places. In some areas of the country, English signs have been replaced with ethnic language signage. All of this is done based upon the constitutional freedom of speech.

What most Americans expect is sensible immigration policies that would place the onus of adaptation on the immigrant and not the citizen. Immigrants should learn how to speak and write the English language, and recite the pledge and national anthem. Immigrants should know what makes America great and protect its greatness. The country looks nothing like it was twenty-five years ago. If immigrants cannot respect America, one has to question if they belong here, or why they want to be here.

3. System dependency versus self-productivity

This is a big issue because current immigration policies allow people who would be considered indigent into the country. Many of these people reach our borders and bring tremendous needs with them. They are unable to be productive or provide for themselves. The cost of this dependency is passed onto the American citizen in the form of more taxes, less federal services, military cutbacks, higher deficits, and uncontrolled spending. Soft immigration policies are eroding the foundation for individual self-productivity.

System dependency is putting additional pressure on the working class. The idea that Americans can absorb the additional costs associated with unrestrained immigration is a poorly founded argument. America is a land of immigrants who have consolidated their strengths, abilities, and productivity into a collective base of self-producing citizens.

Adding people into the country who add to the dependent class of society, while lacking few tangible motivations to better their lives through self-productivity, is a dangerous political experiment. People who are system-dependent have little motivation to improve themselves. They can maintain their culture, language, and lifestyle while receiving federal, state, and local services and funds. There is no need or motivation for system-dependent people to function as self-productive Americans.

4. Lesser element versus contributor

America was built on the ideal that people coming into this country had to provide for themselves and not be provided for by others. The notion was that, as people came into the country, they would help preserve it by working, paying taxes, involving themselves in their community, and discovering solutions that made life better. There was a community expectation that compassion was a limited solution and that becoming a contributor to society was the ultimate goal.

However, compassion immigration has created a new set of challenges. America is accepting an element of people who sustain themselves through crime, gang association, and illegal activity. Their contribution to America is to feed the base desires of humanity. This, in turn, produces subcultures attracting and shielding an element of humanity that is more aggressive, prone to violence, and dangerous for communities. This element demands a loyalty to their subculture that competes against being a contributor to society.

Contributors bring value that is reproducible. They build ideas, possibilities, and hope. Contributors go further than just providing a current tax base or employment opportunities. Contributors bring out the best in others and challenge people to become better in each area of their lives. Contributors do exactly what their label says: they contribute value to their own future and the future of others.

5. *Permanent legal status versus citizenship*

There is a real debate as to how much society must conform to benefit illegal immigrants by providing legal status. Some states are allowing illegal immigrants to hold driver's licenses and specialty vocational licenses, while others prohibit such matters. The argument from the left is that legal status brings illegal immigrants out of the shadows so they can be counted, tracked, and identified. But doesn't the very essence of this argument undermine what constitutional freedoms are about? Doesn't this type of system produce a class of people who have some but not all the freedoms of America? Is this type of status congruent with American ideals and ideology? If it is not, then America has to change its standard for citizenship or enforce its law and policies. This attempt to find middle ground may undo the system for all immigrants and all citizens.

What's at Stake

The real issue is the political comfort zone of the American voting populace. Politicians know there is a limit as to how far they can influence or drag the voting population toward these ideas. It's as if there is an unseen pressure upon voting citizens to accept the confluence of soft immigration for the many illegal immigrants who are within our borders and arriving daily.

However, for those who have come in legally from other countries, acquiring green cards and right to work permits, there is very little consideration given to their plight. Furthermore, political administrations and, most recently, the Obama administration has been very selective as to the country of origin of the immigrants. Most recently, immigrants who are from socialistic or dictatorial countries have been more favored than those from democracies. It's as if there is a direct strategy to import a preselected voter mentality through immigration policy. The unreported truth is that political administrations influence the future voting constituency by exercising immigration policy.

America is at a crossroads of fundamentally transforming its immigration policies without a vote or legislative action. Failing to act is still an act; it's a decision with soiled consequences. The result will be a new citizenry that does not speak our common English language, much less read or write it. This new citizenry will gather and assimilate into their own people-group culture, thereby not embracing the historical and democratic functions of our republic. A citizenry that cannot read the Constitution in English cannot hold government accountable to it.

The end result is that by the next few succeeding generations, a citizenship will dominate the polls that has no understanding of the Constitution, the Bill of Rights, personal freedoms, or government restraints. The American dream will be gone. The constitutional foundations of our country will be severely damaged, if not destroyed completely.

Transforming immigration policy is part of transforming America. Once America looks like every other nation on the face of the earth, our posture as a world leader fades into the annals of history. It is an experiment that can never be undone. Immigration policy is the one policy that determines the future of America.

THE JESUS FACTOR

With all of that stated, there is still a question as to how Christ-followers approach the issue of immigration as an informed citizenry and capable Americans. How should we respond to this issue? What exactly is the Jesus factor as it relates to immigration?

Looking at the Bible as a historical text, and considering world history itself, this is what we know about Jesus and the Jewish people.

1) Jesus was an immigrant. In John 18:36, Jesus was asked by Pilate during His criminal trial if He was King of the Jews: "Jesus answered, 'My Kingdom is not an earthly kingdom. If it were, my followers would fight to keep me from being handed over to the Jewish leaders. But my Kingdom is not of this world'" (NLT).

Notice the clarity in the response of Jesus. He did not seek to identify with the Jewish nation of that time, nor did He claim them as His own people. He did not even dispute the authority of Rome. His simple statement was "My Kingdom is not an earthly kingdom." Jesus is intentionally stating that He is an immigrant. But not only was Jesus a heavenly immigrant who left heaven for earth, He was also an earthly immigrant who left Bethlehem for Egypt.

Immigration saved the life of Jesus. The anti-immigration crowd may reject this fact, but it is true and accurate nonetheless. When the wise men showed up at the door of Jesus's home, they brought three expensive gifts: gold, frankincense, and myrrh. These gifts most likely became the resources that sustained this young family while they lived as immigrants in Egypt. The gifts do not show up again in Scripture; they were probably divine provision for Jesus and His family.

There are a few more truths that need to be stated.

- Jesus did not remain in Egypt, but returned to His homeland.

- Egypt was for his protection, but He brought His own provision.

- Egypt was prophetically linked to Jesus, but not politically linked to Jesus.

There may be a need for people to flee to America for protection from death, but the eventual decision may be for them to return to their homeland. America is not for everyone; global population statistics prove that very point. It could be God is sending millions of people into our nation as a remnant. If so, this would not be the first time in human history God has done this. God is always preserving and redeeming people groups. Historically, cross-culture immigration has been part of God's preservation and redemption plan. However, if divine intent is to return them to their homeland or have them remain here within our borders, then the church must get active in reaching and discipling these immigrants while they are in America.

2) Jesus grew up in a Jewish culture that was overtly governed by Rome (Matt. 5—7; 5:41). Jesus understood a complicated geopolitical society. He interfaced and connected with people in both realms. He grew up oppressed by Roman occupation. Seeing soldiers on the streets, military displays of strength, and continuous signs of Rome's political clout was part of His childhood. Jesus was very aware of Rome, but He focused on His Jewish roots.

He knew how to read and write Hebrew; He spoke Armenian and understood Greek. His was a multicultural world with a singular focus. As a secular tradesman, His relationships, education, and religious practices were rooted in His culture, but everything else pivoted around Rome.

How oxymoronic to think that the Savior of the world who came to redeem the oppressed grew up under oppression.

Jesus had to open His world to the people who occupied it. Although as a people group, the Jews maintained their own traditions and customs, Jesus knew what the non-Jewish world looked like as well. He operated under oppression. How oxymoronic to think that the Savior of the world who came to redeem the oppressed grew up under oppression. The King of kings was oppressed by those who would eventually bow before Him. He truly suffered all things for all humankind, even things relating to the geopolitical spectrum (Heb. 4:15).

The one attribute that sticks out the most is that Jesus remained secure in His divine identity. While others questioned His authority, genealogy, and identity, Jesus was secure and did not retaliate when criticized or rebuffed. He knew He came from the Father and would return to the Father (John 13:1).

3) Jesus established the church to connect with people, within their culture and beyond. The church is an instrument of kingdom dominion designed to influence people, cultures, and governments (Matt. 28:19). Salvation was established through an oppressed people, who were immigrants from Egypt and had historically migrated back to their homeland from Assyria and Persia.

God divinely uses political leaders and governments to shift populations through invasion, war, compassion, economic expansion/contraction, and global strategies. Because God is over all the peoples on the face of the earth, He works through human systems and governments to bring people and nations into cultures where they can hear about Jesus Christ and His kingdom message. What is currently a frustration to millions of Americans may be a divine opportunity for the church, ordained by God.

When a nation tries its best to stop something and fails, perhaps God is in the results. If the twelve sons of Jacob had not immigrated to Egypt, there would be no Israel today. God uses immigration to change the nations, and God uses His church to speak to the nations and proclaim Christ. No matter your position on immigration, certainly there can be an agreement to optimize this opportunity for kingdom advancement.

Salvation was released through a culture and a people divinely purposed for its message. The salvation message was given for all people, for all times, through a divine process. That process historically used immigration to provide, preserve, and create perseverance across Israel. Perhaps the church should seek God passionately and habitually to discover what God wants to release upon the earth through the current immigration excesses in America.

4) From the destruction of Jerusalem in 70 AD until 1948, the entirety of the Jewish population was immigrants. Scripture uses two words to convey immigration: stranger and alien. An alien was a guest in the country; this implied a non-permanent status according to Deuteronomy 24:14. A stranger was one who could freely sojourn through the country; this implied a permanent status according to Leviticus 19:34. The reason God commanded Israel to be kind to aliens and strangers was that

Israel's history and their future pivoted on immigration. They were writing their own future by the way they handled their present situation. This scripture states that God looks after aliens and strangers and will hold us accountable as to how we treat them.

This chapter is not placing political targets on anti-immigration voters. Many believe in strong border protection and effective immigration policies. However, it is a chapter that provides some perspective regarding this issue. The real question is this: How should Christ-followers biblically respond to the issues of immigration and immigrants?

The Bible provides six governing principles that direct believers regarding the issue of immigration:

1. Don't take advantage of them (Deut. 24:14).

2. Show them kindness in their circumstance (Heb. 13:2; 3 John 1:5).

3. Love them as people (Lev. 19:34).

4. Share Christ with them as it is possible (Matt. 28:19).

5. Sow into God's purpose over them (Eph. 2:10).

6. Pray for those who have been given responsibility for deportation, placement, or judicial affairs function (Rom. 13:3).

There are no clean-cut answers to the social issues created by such failed immigration policies over the last twenty-five years. However, perhaps these six points provide a matrix as to how Christ-followers can respond. A framework built with clarity, wisdom, and divine providence by the church is the best alternative to failed political immigration policies.

Chapter 6

I DO

N O MATTER WHICH side you may find your-
self, marriage has become much more complicated in America since the Supreme Court ruled
in 2015 that same-sex marriage is legal in all fifty states.
What first began as a battle between individual rights and
then progressed to states rights has become so much more
than that over time. In the absence of clear moral understanding and principle-centered leadership in government
and the courts, this decision of same-sex marriage came
down to fairness, the inferred right to dignity, and the full
legal rights associated with marriage.[1]

Granted, the legalization of same-sex marriage by the
Supreme Court was a crushing defeat for traditional marriage between a man and a woman and the legal rights
thereto. However, looking back and reflecting it may have
been the religious, traditional marriage proponents that
created the scenario and political climate that eventually
played out in the culture and the courts. The way Christian
leaders responded to this issue and to the gay community
itself may have invalidated its own voice against same-sex
marriage.

The battle *for* homosexual marital rights began in the
1960s. The battle *against* homosexual marital rights began
to get political and religious traction in the late 1970s and
early 1980s. While the Christian community depended
on federal and state laws to protect traditional marriage,

the church as a whole ineffectively dealt with the issues of sex, marriage, divorce, and broken families. The church struggled to communicate the beauty of spiritual intimacy to an emerging "youth" culture. Most Christian leaders refused to address the questions associated with a new generational morality. Questions pertaining to sexual touching, oral sex, intercourse, and same-sex attraction were deemed inappropriate by many believers and church leaders. This was clearly an awkward, painful conversation the church was not ready to discuss or enjoin.

The church held back teaching teens and young adults how to harness their newly discovered awakening of sexual attraction and curiosity until marriage. The church did not give an explanation as to why premarital sex was wrong or a sin. There was little teaching on marriage being a covenant and intercourse being the physical consummation of that covenant. The response regarding sex before marriage was "*No!* Because God said so." This was an insufficient answer to a curious generation.

The substantive questions surrounding same-sex relationships would have to wait. Laws upholding traditional marriage between a man and a woman would have to be defended within the culture and in its politics because the church was too distracted and splintered from sex, marriage, divorce, and family issues. If the church lacked the confidence and substance to address sexual intimacy, marital issues, and divorce, then there was no possible way it had the confidence, substance, and theology to address same-sex marriage. The church was falling behind the culture, fighting a war that did not exist and losing the war that was being fought in front of it.

The American church was breaking apart across the theology of marriage and divorce. Its inability to biblically navigate Christians to respect and redeem marriage would prove to be its downfall in the future argument against same-sex marriage. The church never found the scriptural substance for protecting marriage, and it did not find its voice in this issue. The answer to the arguments of divorce and same-sex marriage was often "because God said so." That answer was not enough for a society pivoting away from the Bible and the church. When the church could not honestly answer questions from society, society quit asking the church for answers.

At the same time, national Christian leaders were unable to articulate their position against same-sex relationships and marriage without invoking ostentatious condemnation upon opponents. Language and terms that resembled righteous vitriol was the public image of Christian America against homosexuality. The church lacked calm, intelligent voices of substance and common sense to address the issues of gayness in America. Condemnation, judgment, and rejection would become the church's voice to gay Americans.

This judgmental position from the 1980s was replayed over and over again by the secular media. Unfortunately, this image would stick to the church and unravel its influence with succeeding generations of Americans. The church that could not protect and preserve traditional marriage was losing its credibility and voice against same-sex marriage. It was not noticeable then, but within twenty-five years the church would either have to compromise with gay theology or battle against being ostracized by the culture. But we are getting ahead of history, so let's take a trip back in time to five decades ago.

It was the late 1960s, and America was thrust into a counter-cultural revolution. Young adults were shifting away from their conservative upbringing and merging into a larger movement. This movement focused on communal adventure, spiritual essence, Mother Earth, ecology, civil rights, political distrust, anti-authoritarianism, social disobedience, war protests, pharmaceutical experimentation, musical expression, and lots of sex. The '60s generation basically shredded all national, political, religious, racial, cultural, and sexual boundaries that had existed in America for the last century. The pioneering anti-culture activities of this generation would become the template for social and political activism forty years later.

To the 1960s generation, sexual barriers were perceived to be something created from the political and religious establishments. Rules were meant to be broken; sexual experimentation was natural; freedoms were more valued than restraints. This would be the generation that would bring LSD, Quaaludes, marijuana, and cocaine into the cultural mainstream. They would embrace new deviances and aggressively accept pornography, abortion, STDs, birth control, homosexuality, and group sex into the mainstream culture of America. Nothing seemed off limits or out of bounds in this generation.

This generation was angry at the established, authoritarian culture of their post-World War II parents. They came of age watching their president get assassinated, lived out their formative years watching a cold war between America and Russia, and feared an atomic or nuclear annihilation. This was the generation that watched the fight for civil rights from the comfort of the living room on their television. Their schools practiced bombing drills. The Korean conflict had just ended, and the military draft was sending America's boys into the Vietnam war to be killed or wounded by the thousands. The 1960s would end as tumultuously as it began; this was the generation who had no hope.

The '70s were tumultuous as well. The beginning of the

decade brought the end of the Vietnam War, the beginning
of legalized abortion, the start of Watergate, and the resig-
nation of President Nixon from the fear of Congressional
impeachment. An oil embargo would create long lines and
higher prices at the gas pump. America's energy policy
would vacillate, causing many people to lose their jobs
or experience career reductions. The stock market fizzled,
and consumer interest rates soared. America would return
the international rights to control the Panama Canal
back to Panama. The American Embassy in Iran would
be taken over, setting up an American hostage crisis that
lasted 444 days.

The country desperately needed to laugh again. While
parents looked to entertainers like Archie Bunker, Sonny
and Cher, Carol Burnett, Lawrence Welk, Bob Hope, Bill
Cosby, and Johnny Carson, their children were turning to
Elton John, Black Sabbath, The Eagles, Journey, the Bee-
Gees, Rod Stewart, and Pink Floyd. Entertainment was
now moving from a family venue to a generational venue.
Drugs, sex, and rock music were synonymous terms. New
cultural algorithms were destroying what had been known
as the traditional fabric of America.

Women were now entering the workforce at an escalated
rate, fast food was coming of age, and cultic expressions of
art and music were sweeping the country. Rock music, R
& B, disco, and electric symphonic sounds were all gen-
erating musical interest simultaneously. Extramarital
workplace affairs were on the rise. Women felt both voca-
tionally independent and suppressed which gave birth to
national women's movements that pushed for equal workplace rights.

In the American home, dual income marriages were
trending but so was divorce. Public schools introduced
sex education courses, and the latch-key generation was

coming of age. The traditional home life of the American family was rapidly changing.

The end of the '70s and early '80s brought about convenient accessibility to porn magazines, cable TV, and the acceptance of seedy movies for private, in-home entertainment. Teenagers would wait for parents to fall asleep so they could sneak downstairs to watch adult-oriented movies on cable. Home delivered issues of pornographic magazines fell into the hands of curious children and teens.

While parents were at work, unsupervised teens would invite friends over to look at porn and invade the private liquor stash of their parents. By the end of the '80s decade, teen alcoholism would be considered a syndrome, teen pregnancy would become an epidemic, and teen suicide would become a cultural signature of generational despair. The pleasures of the parent's generation had become the scourge of their children's generation.

The 1980s and early '90s brought about a new cultural tension regarding sex. Rock musicians, athletes, politicians, and entertainers were being exposed as homosexuals. Homosexuality was considered a lifestyle of choice, and gay people were encouraged to "come out of the closet" and show their pride. During the same time period, male homosexuals were determined to be medically responsible for bringing HIV and AIDS into the mainstream of the "gay" population. There was a real public disdain toward same-sex oriented people. Many in the religious realm considered AIDS a divine judgment against the same-sex lifestyle.

Being gay was considered an elective choice until the late '80s when state, district, and county courts began to rule against gay people in discrimination suits. The fear of AIDS was real as was the fear of a national AIDS epidemic.

Scientific researchers were working around the clock trying to determine how HIV and AIDS were spread. Holding back mainstream homophobia and paranoia was critical and difficult. Some courts ruled that employers who terminated employment with gays had the legal right because homosexuality was a choice, and it was not a protected civil right due to birth, race, origin, or gender For gays, coming "out of the closet" actually meant being shoved out of the workforce and possibly out of society.

From that moment on, frantic searches within some sympathetic legal communities began to find the best legal cases for lawsuits that favored gay progress; these cases, if possible, would be filed in the most sympathetic judicial jurisdictions. Any case that was lost would be appealed while protests were occurring outside the courts with the media reporting. As these cases moved from state courts to federal courts, the gay community found new advocates and support to overturn previous state decisions through the federal process.

Scientists, universities, and research groups were asked to solve this crisis. They were asked to find a cure for AIDS and also asked to look for the existence of a "gay gene." If there was a "genetic tendency" toward same-sex attraction, the gay lifestyle could be protected under the Civil Rights Act of 1964 as a condition at birth. Gays needed civil protection and medical advancements, or they would be wiped out. The battle to survive was on, and the gay movement refused to go away quietly.

Gay activists began touting that they were gay by birth and "God made me this way." The media and Hollywood elites were recruited to message support to the gay community and marginalize how gay people were depicted on the movies screens and televisions across America. Any

person or group who applied resistance to gay progress
was framed as haters, bigots, and idiots.

In retaliation for gay discrimination, many radical gays
intentionally donated their infected HIV blood to dona-
tion centers for the express purpose of infecting "straight"
America, thus creating a dire need for "straight" America
to solve the AIDS crisis. As long as AIDS only infected gay
people, it would be deemed the judgment of God and the
"penalty in their body for their sin," according to Romans
1:27. As long as it was a gay disease, there was little public
motivation to cure the disease. AIDS had to move from
being a gay disease to being a global disease for any significant efforts to be made for a cure.

In 1993, a national gay platform was launched to bring
gayness into the mainstream of society. Part of the platform strategy was to inject the term *gay* into public dialogue to replace the ardent disgust associated with the
word *homosexual*. Gay pride was in, and homosexuality
was out. The gay citizens of America were in a public relations battle that they could not afford to lose. They would
work to make being gay an accepted lifestyle in society,
knowing if they lost this cultural battle it would be lost for
generations.

Also in 1993, there was a national reaction to a ruling by
the Supreme Court of Hawaii. This ruling held the State
must show a compelling interest to prohibit same-sex marriage. In response to the Hawaiian Supreme Court decision, the Federal Defense of Marriage Act, referred to as
DOMA, was passed by Congress in 1996. DOMA passed
with veto-proof margins and was signed into law in 1996
by President Bill Clinton. When it seemed like federal law
would protect the culture from same-sex marriage, the
church's teaching on these issues began to evaporate from
pulpits and Sunday school classes across America.

In the 1990s, the church was still dealing with issues related to divorce and the failure of traditional marriages; clearly it was not ready to deal with same-sex couples or marriage. The focus of the church in the 1990s and early 2000s was on divorce recovery and family healing. Preaching about and promoting Christian marriage with values of fidelity and faithfulness was perceived by some as judgmental and condemning. The eventual result was that the church's voice on marriage values and family traditions would be delegated to conferences, special classes, or premarital counseling.

While traditional marriage seemed to prevail in the legislature, the proponents battling for same-sex marriage were working even harder to breach any legislation on local, county, or state levels. New cases of gay-discrimination, disparity, and inequity were being discovered every day, and new appeals were being filed in county, district, state, and federal courts in continuous fashion. The battle was going into new battlegrounds, but this time the media and the press would be sympathetic toward same-sex causes.

The gay movement was now fighting for its survival, but fortunately for this movement, a newly elected president named Bill Clinton would embrace their cause. Bill and Hillary Clinton reached out to gay coalitions and the LGBT movement as a political symbol of tolerance and political correctness. The national backlash was severe as the liberal social policies of the Clintons would cost their party the control of the House of Representatives. It was the first time in forty years the republicans were in control, and the "People's House" would attempt to refrain and restrain the Clinton administration from the "perversion of America."

However, one of the last executive orders of President Clinton in June 2000 was to declare the month of June

Gay Pride Month in America. Perhaps this was political
retaliation or the Clinton's political evolution on the LGBT
issues. It definitely was a sign of political support for the
causes within the LGBT community.

The battle for gay-normalization began to be waged at
every level. Hollywood stars, entertainers, musicians, athletes, clergy, politicians, and social icons began to either
admit they were gay, support a close relative or friend who
was gay, or vocalize empathy toward the gay community.
Although the American Psychiatric Association removed
homosexuality as a disorder or mental illness in the early
to mid-1970s, Americans were not accepting this position.
So the American Psychological Association released the
following positions in 1994:

> The American Psychological Association released a
> Statement on Homosexuality in 1994—July. Their
> first two paragraphs are: The research on homo-
> sexuality is very clear. Homosexuality is neither
> mental illness nor moral depravity. It is simply the
> way a minority of our population expresses human
> love and sexuality. Study after study documents the
> mental health of gay men and lesbians. Studies of
> judgment, stability, reliability, and social and voca-
> tional adaptiveness all show that gay men and les-
> bians function every bit as well as heterosexuals.
>
> Nor is homosexuality a matter of individual
> choice. Research suggests that the homosexual ori-
> entation is in place very early in the life cycle, pos-
> sibly even before birth. It is found in about ten
> percent of the population, a figure which is surpris-
> ingly constant across cultures, irrespective of the
> different moral values and standards of a particular
> culture. Contrary to what some imply, the incidence
> of homosexuality in a population does not appear
> to change with new moral codes or social mores.

Research findings suggest that efforts to repair homosexuals are nothing more than social prejudice garbed in psychological accoutrements.

In 1994—August, The APA sent a proposal to one of its committees that would declare as unethical the attempts by a psychologist to change a person's sexual orientation through therapy, or referral of a patient to a therapist or organization who attempts to change people's sexual orientation.[2]

This professional position bolstered the theory that homosexuality was a genetic selective orientation, not an elective orientation. It should be noted that according to "The Atlantic" periodical, written by Ed Young dated October 10, 2015 in an article titled "No, Scientists Have Not Found The 'Gay Gene'" that there is still no scientific or genetic proof that sexual orientation, particularly "gay orientation" is a matter of being born gay.[3] Society had bought into a lie that one is born with a specific sexual orientation.

Again, this theory was contrived based upon the gay community losing local and state court cases, which determined that choosing a homosexual orientation was not an activity protected under civil rights law unless it was related to origin at birth. All of the data so far is chasing a theory. There is no scientific proof a person is born gay.

While this was occurring, religious "straight" America fought the gay community in other areas that were rights given to American citizens through the Constitution, Bill of Rights, and federal law—and not based on sexual orientation. The majority of gay couples were seeking the same federal rights and legal privileges for a domestic partner as heterosexual married couples received. Some also sought adoption rights for parenting purposes.

A minority of states had passed legislation allowing for

legal domestic partnerships, also called civil unions, but these laws had no effect on the federal laws exempting gay couples. As these legislative ideas were discussed in other states, religious conservatives attacked these ideas, claiming it would open the door for same-sex marriage. In the absence of not providing any citizen rights (which are obligatory to U.S. citizens), gay couples attacked traditional marriage, making the case that equal love demands equal rights.

Ultimately, in less than twenty years, the Defense of Marriage Act passed by Congress in 1996 failed to defend marriage. The heart of the DOMA legislation was struck down by the Supreme Court in 2013. This ruling dealt with extending federal employee benefits to domestic partners in the same way that these benefits were extended to spouses in traditional marriages. In June 2015, the U.S. Supreme Court agreed in a 5–4 decision to legalize same-sex marriage, thus making same-sex marriage legal in the U.S. and its territories. Now the country is faced with accepting gay marriage.

Most conservative Christians are opposed to gay marriage, while other Christians are resolutely conflicted regarding it. Some of the more theologically liberal or progressive denominations, churches, and spiritual leaders have stated publicly their support for gay marriage, and some support and ordain gay clergy. The American public is now experiencing constitutional and religious tension beyond expression.

The constitutional principles that have served, protected, and built this great democracy are at incredible risk of imploding upon one another in a political fracas. This ruling by the Supreme Court did more than infer dignity and equality to same-sex couples regarding marriage. This ruling invalidated state constitutions, redefined the meaning of the term "family," and all laws, codes, and regulations pertaining to marriage and family. This ruling changed legal benefits, beneficiaries, estate law, end of life rights, adoption laws, and other state and federal boundaries. It has brought confusion to the once-clear principles of freedom of religion and speech.

This ruling has set up constitutional preferences and conflicts that will be battled out in the courts for decades. Attached to the issues of equality and dignity are matters pertaining to the transgender population, and the interpretation that a felt, self-identified orientation is now equal to a true birth orientation. The media has reported that new legal challenges are being considered for adult-child marriage, multiple partner marriage, and animal marriage. Pedophiles are promoting the mantra, "I was born this way," to challenge local laws of indecency and lewd acts with minors.[4] Both the ACLU and the NY Times have argued for equal right for pedophiles.[5] As with all sexual deviances, making room for one opens the door for many more. America is watching laws based on Judeo-Christian morality succumb to laws based on new humanistic morals and ethics. As the courts make legal room for humanistic theories and behavioral sciences to challenge laws and statutes, many more constitutional conflicts will arise.

It is within this environment and this season of humanity that God has placed the church to bring light, truth, healing, and wisdom to a divided nation. Finding truth in the last three decades has been extremely difficult as moral responsibilities crash against constitutional freedoms, rights, and liberties. Yet in this morass of confusion, Jesus speaks.

WHAT JESUS WANTS US TO KNOW

Christ-followers are in the world, but not of the world. Sometimes the tension between these two realms and their driving principles are challenging to navigate. We live in a world that translates personal acceptance into approval. The converse is also true; the lack of acceptance is perceived as disapproval, which is often construed as hatred.

Additionally, it's not the responsibility of the church to condone the behavior and attitudes of the culture. The church has never been culturally correct. From its beginning recorded in Acts 2 and going forward, the church was born and raised in an anti-Christ, anti-church culture and was usually considered a political enemy from its inception. Nothing has changed about the church being outside of the culture in over two thousand years. Even now, the American Church is only beginning to experience what the global church has endured since its beginning. Rarely does the message of the church coincide with the behavior and attitudes of secular culture.

But what the church and Christ-followers are called to do is to interface with the culture. We are to find ways to bridge the gap of tension and unbelief and to point people to their Redeemer, Jesus Christ. Cultural tensions should not mollify and soften our beliefs; rather, they should motivate and poise our convictions and beliefs.

Jesus taught with words that drew bold lines.... He drew bold lines softly, and He spoke stringent truths with gentleness.

Because of cultural tension, it is imperative believers know what they believe and why they believe it. This requires a new and passionate literacy of the Bible and a devotion to prayer. In the absence of the knowledge of God, there is no belief. In the absence of belief, there is no conviction. In the absence of conviction, there is no passion.

In the absence of passion, there is no life-changing message. In the absence of a life-changing message, the heart of people grows cold and hard. True life change and culture change occurs when believers know what they believe, why they believe it, and they act on their beliefs through intercessory wisdom.

Jesus taught with words that drew bold lines. He constantly referred to the written law and words of God. Jesus broke off the additional oral teachings that were attached to the Scripture and the prophets throughout time. He shattered Jewish traditions that had been handed down for generations, traditions that were good but were not from God. Jesus shared God's standards with people, but He packaged His words with wisdom and compassion. He drew bold lines softly, and He spoke stringent truths with gentleness. He embraced the fullness of truth and delivered it in understandable ways, palatable to humanity.

Better to Not Marry?

The teaching of Jesus regarding marriage in Matthew 19 does not coincide with contemporary American marriage values. Jesus taught that marriage was not built upon the attribute of love, the principle of compatibility, or the ethic of sexual fulfillment. Jesus taught marriage was constructed by covenant, over the framework of the Jewish law. Therefore, the teaching of Jesus did not endorse, accept, or tolerate adultery, homosexuality, effeminate genderism, transgenderism, or pedophilia. Anything outside of opposite-gender marriage was unholy and judged as immoral.

People who claim same-sex marriage is acceptable to God because God is love error greatly. They have misconstrued the attribute of God's love to be equal or greater than the character-driven disposition of God's holiness.

God does not change over time. He is consistently constant and never changing (Mal. 3:6; Heb. 13:8).

God's love provided the grace His holiness demanded. Love is the invitation to eternity with God, but holiness is the bridge. Love lacking holiness is incomplete and unable to save (Rom. 6:22; 2 Cor. 7:1; 1 Thess. 4:3-7; Heb. 12:14). Jesus did not come only to convey the love of God, but also to transform us into the holiness of God (Eph. 4:24; 1 Thess. 3:13). Even the Spirit of God, whom God sent to the earth, is referred to as the *Holy* Spirit (John 14:26).

Furthermore, the teaching of Jesus regarding marriage was stricter than that taught by the Apostle Paul in 1 Corinthians 7. Jesus was speaking to a nation whereas Paul was teaching new believers in the church, many of whom were non-Jewish converts in culturally dysfunctional marriages. Jesus taught that marriage was built on the exchange of covenant, not the expression of a legal writ or contract. Jesus would not accept any other viewpoint or perspective; marriage was and is a covenant relationship. Jesus set the standard for the divine intent of marriage; He did not lessen it because the culture had cheapened it.

In Matthew 19:3-10, Jesus laid out what was considered a politically incorrect statement about marriage to the Jewish generation and culture. Even so, how much more does our culture struggle with this passage today? Look at this interaction between Jesus and the Pharisees.

> Some Pharisees came and tried to trap him with this question: "Should a man be allowed to divorce his wife for just any reason?" "Haven't you read the Scriptures?" Jesus replied. "They record that from the beginning 'God made them male and female.' And he said, 'This explains why a man leaves his father and mother and is joined to his wife, and the two are united into one.' Since they are no longer

two but one, let no one split apart what God has joined together." "Then why did Moses say in the law that a man could give his wife a written notice of divorce and send her away?" they asked. Jesus replied, "Moses permitted divorce only as a concession to your hard hearts, but it was not what God had originally intended. And I tell you this, whoever divorces his wife and marries someone else commits adultery—unless his wife has been unfaithful." Jesus' disciples then said to him, "If this is the case, it is better not to marry!" (NLT)

To appreciate this conversation, it's helpful to realize the Pharisees were religious lawyers who combed through the law given to Moses found in the Old Testament books of Exodus, Leviticus, and Deuteronomy. These Pharisees looked for legal issues and entanglements, cultural interpretations and legal opinions to add new traditions and extensions to the law. Their unspoken goal was to make Jewish existence so complicated that the Jews would always need to consult the Pharisees.

In the culture and times when Jesus walked the earth, the tradition upheld by the Pharisees was that a man could divorce his wife for any reason, as long as he provided her with a writ of divorce. After divorcing her with a legal writ, he was free to remarry again. This was a common practice in Israel during the time of Christ. It was also common for men to have more than one wife, as well as to acquire a wife for a specific family or economic purpose and then divorce her. It often turned women toward begging, prostitution, indentured servitude, or slave labor. Although this was a common practice, it was destructive to the Jewish culture, and it was against the Word of God.

When the Pharisees asked this question, they were trying to trap Jesus between an acceptable Jewish custom and the extreme application of the Law of Moses, as Moses was considered the greatest of all Jewish prophets. Without doubt, this question targeted some of the many followers surrounding Jesus. It was hammer time, and Jesus knew His words must be more than descriptive; His response had to be resoundingly definitive and decisive. Jesus would give a prescriptive answer to the sickness of divorce within His culture.

The answer of Jesus is critically important because He goes back to the beginning: the origin of marriage in the Book of Genesis (Gen. 2:22–25). In a theological and hermeneutical context, this is referred to as the "law of first mention." The law of first mention states that the first mention of something in Scripture provides the most accurate context and interpretation. For Jesus to go back to the beginning of humanity is stunning, because He did not start with the Law of Moses, which is where the Pharisees started. Rather, Jesus went to the beginning of time when God made them male and female. This account of the first marriage occurs so early in the Scriptures that the woman has not even been given a name until Genesis 3:20.

Using this example, Jesus cites the actions, words, and intentions of the Godhead relating to marriage. Jesus speaks to marriage as an act between people of the opposite sex, not the same sex; he refers to a man and a woman. When Jesus refers to the two being one, He is referring to covenant consummated through sexual intercourse.

Covenant does not need to be explained in the passage because the listening audience understood completely the context of covenant relationship. This answer from Jesus removed wiggle room for these religious attorneys to use marriage as a convenience for economic, family, pleasure, or political reasons. The point of Jesus is this: no matter what the motivation to get married is, the relationship is a covenant relationship before God and not just a legal contract before man.

COVENANT EXPLAINED

In the Bible, we discover that God does everything on the basis of covenant. Covenant is a spiritual agreement, whereas a contract is a legal agreement. *Covenant* literally means to cut or tear until blood flows. Once the flesh is torn or cut, covenant is sealed by the blood. Covenant requires either the tearing or cutting of the flesh and the presence of blood. If there is no blood, there is no covenant. A contract is sealed by word and does not require blood. Covenant operates by a higher principle than a contract because it requires blood and it produces life.

Biblically, sexual covenant occurs when a female virgin is penetrated the first time by a man, and there is a tearing that occurs in the vaginal area. The hymen is torn, and the woman bleeds. This tearing of flesh and bleeding initiates covenant simultaneously. In this process of creating covenant, two people become one flesh. Out of the "one flesh" process, God brings forth another human life.

In the Jewish culture, there was such value placed on virginity and covenant that when a couple married, the sheets from their sexual copulation could be inspected by her parents if there was an accusation she was not a virgin (Deut. 22:13–21). If there was not a blood-soaked towel or sheet as proof of her virginity from vaginal penetration, she was stoned at the doorposts of her father's house. Covenant, especially blood covenant, was held in high esteem according to Jewish law. Any act that bypassed covenant or could not produce covenant was detestable; therefore, it's called an abomination in Scripture. Homosexual activity cannot produce covenant; therefore, it was considered an abomination (Lev. 20:13).

There are two words that people comingle together regarding unbiblical sexual activity that are completely different in meaning and should not be interchanged. The first is called an abomination and the term "abomination" is always used in conjunction with bypassing covenant activities. In the Hebrew language, *abomination* literally means something that is disgusting—or to loathe something that is an idol or an idolatry (Lev. 20:13).[6] This is the perfect word picture to explain why homosexuality is an abomination before God. In the same way that idolatry bypasses a salvation covenant, homosexuality bypasses a marriage covenant.

The second word is *perversion,* and its Hebrew meaning indicates an unnatural mixture or to confuse things (Lev. 18:23; 20:12).[7] When sexual activity involves incest or animals, it is a perversion or an unnatural mixture that brings confusion. Notice the clear delineation between these acts and these words.

Again, to substantiate this truth, the Antichrist is referred to as "the abomination of desolation" (Mark 13:14, NKJV). Why do Daniel and Jesus refer to the Antichrist this way (Dan. 12:11; Mark 13:14)? Because this false Christ is claiming to be God and bypassing the blood covenant. This is a detestable, idolatrous act. There is no covenant without blood, and anyone who seeks to enjoin spiritual covenant absent of blood is an abomination in God's sight. This is why Jesus offered Himself on the cross, being bloodied and wounded for our sins (Isa. 53:4–11). Without the shedding of blood, there is no remission of sin (Matt. 26:28; Heb. 9:22).

The Book of Malachi is a book about covenant. It is strategically placed as the last book in the Old Testament. More than that, it is the final prophetic word given to Israel before the physical incarnation of Jesus Christ upon the Earth. There is a four-hundred-year period of prophetic silence from the end of Malachi until the manger cry of the newborn Jesus in Bethlehem.

In the Book of Malachi, God speaks about hating the act of divorce. God refers to marriage as covenant in Malachi. Malachi 2:14 specifically refers to the woman as a wife of covenant. According to verse 15, the purpose for this covenant is for the marriage to produce holy offspring or children that come under God's salvation covenant. Malachi 2:16 states that when covenant is broken, God views it as a violent act because, once covenant is created, God binds the man and woman together. Breaking apart what God has sealed as covenant is indeed a violent act. Malachi describes it as violently tearing a garment in half.

To further illustrate breaking a marriage covenant, Jesus states that Moses permitted divorce because their hearts were hard or literally tough and destitute of spiritual perception (Matt. 19:8). This is an indictment about their spiritual condition, their motives, and their view of marital sacredness. Jesus said they sought divorce because they were destitute of spiritual perception; in other words, they could not recognize the value and validity of spiritual covenant. Once their hearts were spiritually hard, there was no other way to redeem the marriage relationship. Thus divorce was permitted, but not divinely preferred.

Jesus stated that although Moses permitted divorce, it still displeased God. He went on to say if there was no act of adultery, divorce was not justified. Only adultery could break covenant while both people were alive. In fact, if a divorce occurred for any other reason other than adultery, God would not consider the covenant broken; He would still see the marriage as intact, and any sexual activity with another person as adultery.

This teaching was so harsh and strong to the Jewish

culture that the disciples agreed that it was better to not marry (Matt. 19:10). This response from the twelve shows how accepted divorce was in their community and how marriage was viewed as burden. Jesus did not excuse divorce in marriage because He respected it as a covenant relationship.

Currently in American culture, marriage is losing its sacredness. It's often mocked in Hollywood and in the entertainment world; it's disrespected and held in contempt in the media. In some activist organizations, marriage is likened to a form of legal bondage; unwanted marital sexual intimacy is classified as marital rape. As the culture embraces more secular values, the meaning of marriage and its spiritual promise continues to diminish. Cohabitation is growing as marriages decrease.

When marriages fail, self-reliance within the broken family becomes more entrenched in the human psyche, and internal walls are often erected for self-preservation. Typically, most people leave a broken marriage more hurt and less trusting. Vulnerabilities increase.

The danger in disregarding traditional marriage is that the values attached to marriage diminish as well. Values like family first, commitment, persistence, dependability, trust, patience, serving, manners, conflict resolution, togetherness, reliability, confidence, sexual fidelity, awareness, and respect become damaged when marriage is disregarded. When these values are not modeled, family members, and especially children, are not positively mentored, nurtured, and developed.

Once marriage is disregarded, it can be redefined, and that is exactly what is happening right now in America. The redefinition of the American family is the essence of national political transformation. It has become the primary formula to assimilating diversity and scattering

predictability. As this redefinition continues to occur, the
unexpected becomes the accepted; stability evaporates,
and division compounds.

Once redefinition occurs, tradition and the values
attached to it fade like a swollen sunset. The former glory
of monogamous, life-long relationships become a comma
in the sentence of humanity. Redefinition creates new
rules in a new culture that has never experienced the light
of a traditional God-defined family.

When covenant marriage is disregarded, society sub-
stitutes dysfunctional relationships in its place. A new
normal forces acceptance of a subculture that abrogates
values like commitment, fidelity, and faithfulness and
replaces them with the ethos of tolerance, fluctuation, and
the common good. In this "new normal" society, marriage is no longer about the establishment of an individual
family holding self-determined values and being func-
tional within a community. Rather, marriage is about the
establishment of a common social mentality, acceptance
of a progressive lifestyle, and the dependency of a community or identity for survival. Redefining marriage is redefining truth for families and politics for America.

The final product of this society is a citizenry so broken
and fragile that any spoken truth that challenges their
reality is rejected and shouted down. Reality is regarded
as the only "known" truth. The ultimate societal consequence is a fascist mentality that suppresses truth, redi-
rects hope, and rejects God.

In the evolution of the American culture, the weakest or
most victimized person will soon be the most celebrated.
The political mantra will move from individual sacrifice of
all to a mantra of all sacrifice for the one. The inversion of
truth has dynamic consequences.

Marriage is being transformed into something that is

unrecognizable, convenient, and limited. The true American dysfunction is that traditional marriage and family values are being replaced by cohabitating couples, same-sex couples, ideological communities, and governmental dependency. You cannot put asunder a generation of marriages without putting asunder a generation of Americans. When the most intimate of all promises can no longer be trusted or valued, little else, if anything, can be trusted.

The ultimate result of this dysfunctional redefinition will be a nation that lacks trust in one another—and lacks confidence in the future and character to establish a meaningful legacy. Life lessons are taught through family structures, not through politically correct social engineering. Human nature has its limits, and the American culture is about to discover those limits.

THE ANSWER IS WISDOM

Perhaps the real questions facing American Christ-followers include the following:

1. How do we respond when our freedom of speech and religion conflicts with the civil and marriage rights of same-sex couples?

2. How do we engage in our freedoms if they conflict with the dignity of same-sex couples?

What is becoming awkwardly obvious throughout America is that the body of Christ was neither prepared nor comfortable with the secularization of the culture. America has become a post-Christian culture, and it's time that the body of Christ adjusted to this change. Remarkably, in the last twenty-five years while believers were having Sunday church, worship services, home groups, fellowship, and patriotic celebrations, the culture shifted around them. Everyone saw this coming except the church. The church maintained its traditions, styles, and principles, believing Jesus would return.

While opinions vary and debates rage regarding secular, humanistic cultural shifts in education, business, entertainment, politics, sports, and government, the truth is that America has changed and Christ-followers have to navigate through this dark culture. This is very similar to the cultural environment Jesus sent the disciples into in Matthew 10. Listen to the stark content of His words: "Behold, I send you out as sheep in the midst of wolves. Therefore be wise as serpents and harmless as doves. But beware of men" (Matt. 10:16–17, NKJV).

Notice the contrast between the two subjects in this verse—sheep versus wolves. Wolves are predators; they will roam for miles across their territory hunting for food. They instinctively move toward fresh prey; whether the prey is on its feet, running away, or frozen in fear, wolves move toward the kill. They attack in packs because they are more successful bringing down a large animal attacking as a group. They look for animals that are distracted, isolated, young, or weak. They have no respect for natural order or for the size of prey; they are driven by instinct and desire. They sense fear and prey on those who are fearful. Wolves love to howl from high places or open spaces. Wolves are highly intelligent and have full sensory perception. Wolves know how to survive; it's their nature.

Sheep, on the other hand, are grazers. They roam a few feet at time. They instinctively locate green grass and have a tendency to eat down into the root. If sheep are not moved from grazing area to grazing area, they will destroy a field's ability to reestablish itself. Sheep have to be sheared; they cannot shear or cleanse their own wool.

Sheep have a much better chance of survival when they have a shepherd.

Sheep are intelligent, but not always intuitive. Sheep flock and follow. They will follow the lead sheep to their own death. Sheep are social and need to see and sense other sheep. They have a great sense of smell and hearing but struggle to see with clarity. They can perceive movement but lack depth of sight or dimensional perception, especially when walking with their heads up. Sheep need to stop and look at things closely. They are afraid of shadows and poorly lit environments.[8]

When Jesus said that we were being sent as sheep, He did not say we would travel without a shepherd. He did say the wolves would be present. So His advice was to be wise as serpents and harmless as doves (Matt. 10:16).

Christ-followers in America seem to be making some foolish decisions, giving unwise responses to a secular culture that has reasoned away their necessity to exist. There is a constant push by same-sex marriage proponents to position Christ-followers to defend their faith against gay marriage. Once this is done, the unsuspecting Christ-follower is painted as an extreme religious fanatic. Notice the gay marriage crowd does not use this tactic against Muslims or Jews, who believe in traditional marriage just as Christians do.

It appears as if radical gay-rights groups are seeking to reshape the constitutional right of religious freedom. This reshaping would include removing it from the public forum and monitoring its private liberty. In time, it could be that this and other freedoms will be subject to civil rights legislation.

If the truth were known, fanatical gay leftists have never sought to take on hard targets like Islam or Judaism. Christianity has always been their target because America was founded on Christian principles. Islamic and Jewish principles are not being attacked. Those religions at times align with Christianity, but those religions do not supply the founding principles of America. This attack is about discrediting founding principles attached to the Constitution and the Bill of Rights that are associated with the Bible and the context of the church.

WISDOM SPEAKS

So how does the body of Christ respond? Christ-followers must become more savvy and wise in dealing with the post-Christian culture. Certainly, as a small-business owner, Jesus dealt with the influence of Rome upon His business. We know Jesus had no issues giving to Caesar what amounted to Rome's share of taxes. This tax money was used to support the agenda and principles of Rome while oppressing the Jewish people. Jesus stated to give to God what belonged to God as well.

Faith and wisdom hold hands. God does not work in one, without working in the other.

There has to be a way for Christians to embrace their God-gifts and release those gifts to a secular society while upholding their faith. Perhaps Christ is allowing this legal and cultural tension to position His body strategically into the areas where the name of Jesus has never been spoken. The counsel of Proverbs 4:7 has never been more applicable than now: "Wisdom is the principal thing; therefore get wisdom. And in all your getting, get understanding" (NKJV).

The time has come for Christ-followers in business and in the culture to think through their faith in the context of wisdom. I remind our congregation repeatedly that faith and wisdom hold hands. God does not work in one, without working in the other.

WHERE TO BEGIN

1. *Value marriage.* If you are married, begin with your marriage. Support traditional marriages between a man and woman. Attend the weddings and marriage celebrations of friends and family members; celebrate anniversaries. Find ways to acknowledge that marriage relationships are more than a legal contract; they are a spiritual covenant. Begin to place spiritual emphasis on marriage in your life, in your conversations, and in society.

2. *Talk to others about the blessing of covenant marriage.* Help single adults recognize that marriage is better than cohabitation. Cohabitation has a higher divorce rate than traditional marriage. Help people realize marriage offers the best partner solutions when it's focused on being a blessing to your mate.

3. *Keep God in the center of marriage.* Emphasize that marriage began as a promise before God. Marriage is recognized by the State because of issues associated with taxes, property ownership and children, but the State did not create marriage; it was created by God. Speak of marriage in terms of covenant and faith. Remind people that marriage is God's plan for families.

4. *Defeat the marriage busters: communication, sex, and money.* When people struggle
to communicate, soulish intimacy struggles.
Spouses need to connect as friends, lovers,
fans, and counselors. Emphasize communication and work on it to keep it healthy. Speak
encouraging words and build one another up.
When people struggle with communication,
they struggle with sex and money manage-
ment. There are great resources available to
help couples in these areas. Find them, use
them, and recommend them.

5. *Commit to a local church.* Yes, wor-
shipping together as couples with other
couples is a huge way to improve your marriage. Spiritual transformation seeps into
marriages.

6. *Select friends who value marriage.* It's
true that your friends will influence you
as you will influence them. Find friends
who believe in the value of marriage. Avoid
spending time with friends who criticize
their spouses or have values that discourage
marital commitment.

7. *Stay faithful to your spouse.* Temptations
to stray from your spouse are continuously
present in this culture. Determine the reasons why fidelity matters in your marriage
and hold to those reasons. You are the best
deterrent to an affair.

8. *Understand and share the purposes of
marriage.* God made marriage for couples to experience the sexual pleasures of

a relationship, to procreate, and to prosper together within the context of His blessings. Understand these purposes, share them with your children and friends, and change the conversation of marriage.

9. *Champion traditional marriage.* It may be that over the next few decades the church is known for traditional ceremonies, instruction on traditional marriages, and family values. If that is the case, what a wonderful indictment or label! Even though culture and national laws have untethered themselves from biblically defined morality, the voice of the church is founded in Scripture, not politics.

10. *Treat those in the LGBTQ community with compassion, respect, and kindness because they are God's children too.* There is no one more committed to the salvation of the lost than Jesus Christ (Luke 19:10). When Christ-followers treat those in the LGBTQ community rudely or harshly judge them, they may think Christ will not accept them either. Treat unbelievers with respect, dignity, and love. The way we love unbelievers, whether in the LGBTQ community or otherwise, communicates that Jesus is compassionate, caring, and forgiving.

When people sin, they don't sin against believers; rather, they sin against God. If God, who has been sinned against, is patient for sinners to repent (2 Pet. 3:9), then the body of Christ should not become a hindrance making it difficult for people to repent. It does not matter what an unbelieving person stands for, stands against, or how they self-identify; people should be treated with dignity, respect, care, and compassion (Eph. 4:32). When those who are unsaved are treated as God's children, often they become open to listen about Jesus or discover faith in Christ. It is possible to show people dignity, respect, care, and compassion without compromising convictions or beliefs. We can accept people as they are without approving of their actions. Jesus did this, and we as Christ-followers can do the same. Unless the church shares the light of Christ with the unbelieving world, their world will remain a spiritually dark place.

For the church to maintain any respect, it must maintain its convictions on traditional marriage. While some denominations are accepting and even endorsing gay nuptials, gay clergy, and gay membership, the denominations that have rejected these things must stand for their beliefs and doctrines. Once the traditional marriage voice leaves the culture, it will be lost for generations. The inconvenience of the church's message is nothing compared to the generational displacement of human values and virtues through its silence.

Once the church begins to value marriage again, it can slowly regain its voice regarding marriage. The laws permitting gay marriage will remain, but that's not the issue. When the church can influence society toward biblical marriage, then people will gravitate toward traditional marriage. Politics follows culture, and culture follows faith. Let faith have its complete work, and the culture can be redeemed.

Chapter 7

THE LEPER ON THE ROAD

P USHED ASIDE. IGNORED. Despised. Feared. Ridiculed. Mocked. Misunderstood. Isolated. Anonymous. Targeted.

These are just a few of the words associated with discrimination. Discrimination takes on many forms and works through subtle tones. Discrimination can operate as a subculture in organizations, corporations, businesses, communities, and churches. Other words that have synonymous application in American culture are the words prejudice, bigotry, and racism.

Not everyone understands the sting of discrimination. While many people experience some form of bias or discrimination within their lifetime, there are entire groups of people who live with it on a daily basis. It's all they know. This is the way society treats them. They are a dreaded interruption. Their life counts for very little. Their communities are neglected. Their future is not empowered. Yet, few in the modern church understand their plight, and even fewer in the modern church respond to it.

For too long, the church in America has embraced a "segregated" faith. This segregation is not just based on skin color or nationality; it's based on economics, physical disabilities, age, status, mentality, culture, and ethnicities. It's been said that Sunday mornings are some of the most segregated hours in America, and the church is proving this fact weekly. Perhaps a reason for this segregation lies within the context and composite of the American Church.

Churches are identified through relational fellowship and spiritual intimacy. It's part of their nature and culture. Church is a place where spiritual connection occurs and the internal bonds of humanity emanate. Soulish transparency and spiritual rituals create adhesive relationships that withstand time, adversity, and change. However, what the church has enjoyed as a means of spiritual intimacy has also coerced the church away from influencing the American culture with regard to discrimination.

It's somewhat oxymoronic that the chemistry within the local body of Christ has often been toxic with regard to healing the prejudicial marrow of its surrounding communities. Many churches and Christ-followers do well in a clandestine, spiritual environment. However, these same churches and believers struggle connecting with their community and neighborhoods. They are in the community but often find themselves outside of the community's culture and heartbeat. They are answering questions no one is asking and stumbling over questions the culture is asking.

The church's influence is being driven away from the culture. This is due in part to its innate rationalization to discriminate through religious separation and racial segregation. Since its inception in the Book of Acts, the church has had to deal with discrimination relating to race, origin, culture, and traditions. When the body of Christ becomes selective in where it goes and who it accepts, the culture rejects the church.

In some ways, discrimination is causing the church to lose its sense of hearing.

As American culture continues to shift to a post-Christian modality, religious discrimination is destroying bridges of trust that connect human beings. It's erasing the lines that could connect society with the church. Culture pivots around what its influential voices are speaking. The church is not consistently listening to or aware of these influential voices. In some ways, discrimination is causing the church to lose its sense of hearing.

To complicate this matter more, the American church is now faced with drawing bold lines in the sands of culture. When lines are drawn and the sand is still shifting, then the church is perceived as an organization of hate or bias. The church looks like a place of disenfranchisement instead of a place of acceptance. Honestly, this is where the church has an image or public relations problem.

In addition to these complexities, many in the body of Christ are comfortable with all Anglo, all African-American, all Hispanic, or all Asian congregations. People prefer to engage in spiritual intimacy within the safe zones of similarity. Similarities such as skin color or language groups, ethnicities, economic backgrounds, social networks, or congruent spiritual beliefs drive the gatherings.

It's interesting that when the tangibles within a church change, it often changes the intangibles. This could be the reason why Sundays in the body of Christ looks less like a body and more like a special interest group. It's astonishing how a worldwide, multicultural body can look one dimensional when it gathers in most neighborhoods.

Are believers more comfortable with discrimination than with God's creative imagination over His church? Is the church comfortable with self-imposed biases? Is this a prejudice that is masked through beliefs? Or is it legitimate transparency among like-minded people?

The culture of America is being redefined continuously,

and there is a real need for the body of Christ to be a steadfast, viable model of faith to the culture. However, in order to be noticed by a post-Christian society, the church will be forced to either adopt positions that challenge its doctrines or voice opposition to the culture.

But perhaps there is another option. That option is to speak and model truth to the culture through a stance of compassion, free of discrimination. It is manifesting the truth in love. It's giving acceptance to people even without approving of their actions.

When truth is given without love, it comes across mean or harsh. When love is given without truth, it becomes deceptive or manipulative. Loving people without condition is the most effective way to influence.

THE LEPER ON THE ROAD

In Matthew 5–7, Jesus shared a compelling discourse that set his listeners' ears on fire. He ended His homily with a real challenge to measure others with a cup of non-judgment and to freely give to others what they expected to receive themselves. His words could not be more defined or deliberate.

At the conclusion of His teaching, an interesting thing happened as Jesus was coming down from the mountain. With hundreds or perhaps thousands of people following Jesus, He was met by a leper who specifically came out of the shadows to worship Jesus. It was in this moment that culture was about to clash with the kingdom principles Jesus had just taught. Take a look at Matthew 8:1–4.

> Large crowds followed Jesus as he came down the mountainside. Suddenly, a man with leprosy approached him and knelt before him. "Lord," the man said, "if you are willing, you can heal me and make me clean." Jesus reached out and touched

him. "I am willing," he said. "Be healed!" And
instantly the leprosy disappeared. Then Jesus said
to him, "Don't tell anyone about this. Instead, go to
the priest and let him examine you. Take along the
offering required in the law of Moses for those who
have been healed of leprosy. This will be a public
testimony that you have been cleansed."

If you're unfamiliar with the life of a leper, check this out:

In biblical times lepers were considered unclean,
and they were forced to separate themselves from
the public. The mere touch of a leper brought
uncleanness, and breathing the same air of a leper
was believed to be dangerous. When someone was
pronounced "leprous," they were looked upon as
dead and cast out of society to dwell in a special
place or colony in the wilderness, living in caves or
tents. In ancient Israel, lepers were commanded to
wear certain clothes, keep themselves a certain distance from people, wear special bells, and they had
to cry "unclean, unclean" if someone was too close
(Lev. 13:45). The rabbis viewed leprosy as a chastise-
ment from God because of moral issues.[1]

Notice what Matthew writes: the leper approached
Jesus. In Jewish society, lepers were a unique class of
people; they were an underclass of society. They lived in
a realm of subjective scrutiny. Their desperate condition
brought instant judgment from society. The assumption
was their physical malady was a divine judgment for their
sin. Engaging or intervening with a leper was frowned on
by the locals. This was an activity that was nearly impossible to do without compromising religious purity, jeopar-
dizing health, or being socially excluded.

In Jewish society, even compassion had its limits when

it involved a leper. Discrimination was viewed as an act of righteous survival. Yet this leper defied all protocol and violated acceptable boundaries. He approached Jesus out of desperation.

Lepers lived a lonely life. They had no home or permanent shelter because it was burned to the ground once they were diagnosed with leprosy. They lived a transient life and stayed wherever they could find lodging, as long as it was outside the city. Their covering was only the clothes on their back. They did not possess the luxury of anonymity.

The emotional toll of leprosy was indescribable. Relational isolation. Survival by begging. Loss of dignity. Humiliation. Lepers lived a life of dependency with very little support. Rejection was their norm.

The mental anguish of leprosy must have been overwhelming. The only people who could accept them were those who were just like them. Simple pleasures, like laughter, family, hugs, kisses, and smiles were distant memories of a different life. Human touch was a lost expression. A diagnosis of leprosy was feared more than death; a leper would lose all the meaning of life before losing life itself. The mental side of this disease was nothing less than cruel.

The economic injustice was severe. This disease robbed the soul. Begging removed all sense of dignity. Insults were as common as lack. Survival was a full-time job for a leper. Their survival depended upon the compassion of a stranger or the fortune of luck. Neither one was a sure bet in Israel.

At first glance, comparing the condition of a leper to prejudice, bigotry, discrimination, or racism may sound like a huge stretch. However, the response of discrimination from one human toward another human is really the raw essence of this comparison. Human nature is the one consistent element in discrimination.

It's human nature to automatically stereotype others. Human nature judges, presumes, and disconnects with people over perceived or tangible differences. This judgmental disposition seems to be an innate response toward people who appear different from us. It's true that some people have stronger tendencies toward discrimination than others. Yet what we have learned is discrimination is a conditioned response that can be reversed.

In order to remove any confusion, the following definitions should bring congruency and clarity to this discussion.

Prejudice is defined as "The act or state of holding unreasonable preconceived judgments or convictions; an adverse judgment or opinion formed unfairly or without knowledge of the facts." A second definition describes *prejudice* as "irrational suspicion or hatred of a particular social group, such as a race or the adherents of a religion."[2]

A *bigot* is defined as "one who is strongly partial to one's own group, religion, race, or politics and is intolerant of those who differ."[3]

Discrimination is defined as "treatment or consideration based on class or category, such as race or gender, rather than individual merit; partiality or prejudice."[4]

Racism is defined as "the belief that race accounts for differences in human character or ability and that a particular race is superior to others." The second definition notes that racism is "discrimination or prejudice based on race."[5]

There was no way to ignore the fact that the Jewish society felt superior to the common leper. There was a great deal of discrimination and prejudice exercised against the leper. Yet, there are great parallels between the response of Jesus to the leper and the way Christ-followers should respond in matters of discrimination, race, prejudice, or bigotry. In this brief passage, Jesus put before us the right way to respond to situations and circumstances that are infused with prejudicial differences, bigoted discrimination, or racial disparity.

Diffusing Disparity

The beginning of this encounter was framed by how *receptive* Jesus was to engage the leper. With a large crowd following Him, Jesus did not respond based upon the expectations of the crowd. Jesus responded to the expectations of the leper. Jesus was all-in when the leper spoke to Him. Jesus did not look around to see who was watching or listening. He did not attempt to placate His followers. Jesus dialed into the conversation with the leper.

What is even more astonishing about this event is it occurs at the beginning of Jesus's ministry. Jesus was comfortable risking the acceptance of the crowd in order to minister to this leper. Obviously, people were watching Jesus. Perhaps some wanted to shun the leper or direct the attention of Jesus elsewhere. Others were probably aghast that Jesus would be so close to this leper as to breathe the same air or touch one another. Jesus never allowed the expectations of others to remove His focus from His purpose. Jesus was receptive and focused.

Then Jesus *listened* to the leper. Granted, it was obvious the leper needed healing, but Jesus dignified his request by not presuming anything. We see this often with Jesus. In Mark 10:51, He asked the blind beggar Bartimaeus, "What do you want me to do for you?" *There is something special about the art of listening that conveys dignity and respect.* Jesus knew what the man needed, but He gave the leper opportunity to speak for himself. Jesus knew that listening brings relief to the soul, and Jesus cared for this man's soul.

Once the man shared his need for healing, Jesus did

something no one could predict, not even the leper. Jesus *responded* to the man by touching him in his leprous condition. Jesus knew that once this man was healed, many people would touch him, hug him, and accept him. *What Jesus focused on was that no one had accepted or affirmed the leper in his current condition.* By touching the leper, Jesus transferred compassion, hope, and acceptance to this beggar.

The leper may have not remembered who touched him after his healing, but he will never forget the touch he received when he was "untouchable." Jesus continued to amaze people by doing the unexpected! According to the law of Moses, when Jesus touched the leper, Jesus was considered unclean. The one who was clean became unclean to make another clean. What a powerful picture of salvation!

But Jesus was just beginning, because the next step was for the man to be completely *transformed.* The words of Jesus were so simple and precise: "I am willing, be healed." Instantly, the man was cured. Sores disappeared; every wound was made whole. Scars were transformed into new skin. Appendages grew back, puss dried up and disappeared, and the terrible odor of disease vanished. Leprosy had been banished from this man. In one moment with Jesus, he was completely transformed.

Can you imagine what it must have been like to witness such a thing? Or better yet, to be on the receiving side of healing? This was truly a miracle that championed the ministry of Jesus and the hope of the oppressed. Just knowing Jesus could do these things began to bring hope to others far away from the miracle. If Jesus did this for one leper, maybe Jesus would do it for another! Hope was lifted high that afternoon.

Then Jesus did something many people do not understand. Instead of allowing the man to celebrate his healing with those nearby, Jesus commanded the former leper to appear before the priest and offer the appropriate sacrifices for healing. Jesus wanted the miracle *confirmed* first before anyone testified.

Jesus knew what the man had experienced. Jesus saw with His own eyes what an incredible miracle occurred. But Jesus would not shortchange the process. The work of God must be confirmed and certified as a credible miracle. When the miraculous was validated as credible, then it could be celebrated.

This part of the story emphasizes the importance of confirmation. Credible validation delivered a testimony of righteousness. When a miracle of this magnitude occurred, only those qualified to judge it were called upon to do so. Because leprosy was considered a "sinner's" disease, the leper was sent to the priest. When the priest judged and confirmed the healing from leprosy, the priest was also declaring that the sin-source that caused the leprosy was gone as well. Healing from leprosy could only occur if the source of sin was removed.

First impressions and the amazement of a crowd were not sufficient to validate this miracle; priestly inspection and an offering accompanied the results. Validation was the source of a celebration of grace. Jesus did not send the leper away to the priest to get him out of the way; Jesus sent him to the priest to confirm he had been forgiven and healed! Confirmation was about to release celebration!

Perhaps it is time that the church began to focus on its purpose in greater detail. The purpose of the church is not to produce theological ideologies, but rather to produce the results of righteousness. The walls surrounding race, bigotry, prejudice, and discrimination will not come down until leaders in the local communities begin to address the fundamental issues of perception, reality, and righteousness.

Avoiding the difficult conversations or acting in accordance with the expectations of the crowd will not bring the changes that are necessary to heal communities. Dialing into the conversations and being present in the dialogue is what is needed and necessary to diffuse the tension developing in this country. Righteousness exalts a nation. In the absence of doing what is right, the offenses of bigotry, discrimination, and prejudice are gaining new strongholds in American society.

Before the Civil War, the church in America remained silent in the matters of slavery, racism, prejudice, and discrimination. Christians would gather to sing southern-styled hymns and praise the Lord, then go back to their farms and plantations and carry on with slavery. After the Civil War, the church tolerated discrimination and prejudice as a fact of life. For the most part, the church did not expect or teach Christians to turn away from racism.

During the racial unrest of the late 1950s and early 1960s, it was the church that often stood in way of civil rights and community transformation. Preachers were more appreciative of people attending a church of their own color. Throughout history, rarely has the church been on the forefront of societal shifts that lessen discrimination.

Race relations, bigotry, discrimination, and prejudice are rising again in a new, younger generation. These disturbing attributes are often embedded with the emotional debris of anger, hatred, and violence. What is rising up in this younger generation is a passion to hate more and to hate deeper. The only thing that can liberate the human heart from such hateful hostility is the grace of Jesus Christ. When grace appears, transformation flows. Grace is the solution that must confront this new generation.

If tolerance could heal a nation, America would
be whole.

This is the moment when history will record the actions
and message of the church. Christ-followers need to begin
listening to the issues that surround their communities
There has to be a receptive response targeted at a younger
generation.

The current secular culture can only lecture on the ethics
of tolerance. If tolerance could heal a nation, America
would be whole. Future generations are waiting for the
body of Christ to spiritually and intellectually address the
issues born from discrimination. This will be a battle in
every emerging generation until the church leads the culture into transformation through biblical truth, not political values.

Church leaders and Christ-followers need to show true
receptivity to the issues surrounding minority populations and neighborhoods. Right now is a good time to
listen to the issues and understand the dilemmas that
exist. Listening is not a response of acceptance, approval,
or sympathy. It is, however, a response that affirms the
dignity of the people affected by these issues. It is the first
step to solve them. Being receptive and listening are the
first steps of grace!

For most white, suburban-dwelling Christ-followers,
racial tension associated with discrimination has been
something watched on television or viewed on the internet.
But with the ever-present media capturing images and
interviews, a digital documentary has been created for
future generations. The future generations of our children and grandchildren in this nation will either see a
church that focused on the needs, issues, and concerns of

discrimination—or swept them under the rug for future generations to work through. These discussions that can heal and transform our communities are not going to be silenced. They cannot be quieted; they can only be delayed.

It would be far better for the church to begin this process now than to wait for a Muslim cleric or Imam to lead the discussion in ten or twenty years from now. The conversation of discrimination is a dialogue that the world will listen to and applaud the church for discussing. If the church remains quiet and self-absorbed and never leads in racial healing and the transformation of discrimination, then the church will be condemned as the history of nations is recorded. Discrimination could be referred to as the elephant in the room or—as in the experience of Jesus—the leper on the road.

The church was called to be ministers of reconciliation (2 Cor. 5:18). One of the purposes of reconciliation is righting wrongs. The past cannot be undone, but it can be forgiven, and the future can be redirected. Proactive measures can be put in place to reshape and renew communities. As long as people look to the federal government to correct abuse or wrongs associated with discrimination, solutions will always be political and temporary.

The church is built on the empowerment principles conveyed to it by its founder, Jesus Christ (Matt. 16:18). The power of heaven is present to heal and transform communities if the leaders of the local church will be receptive to the individuals and issues that need healing. This is an opportunity for the church to redeem its influence in the American culture and the local community.

Furthermore, the church has been given the wisdom of God through the Holy Spirit. One direct advantage of the church convening this conversation is that the church brings God's heavenly wisdom, full of grace, to the conversation. This is the season for Christ-followers to bring wisdom, grace, and solutions to a frustrated citizenry. Society is worn down and worn out from the politics of prejudice, bigotry, discrimination, and racism.

Once answers have been accepted and received, let them be reviewed under the scrutiny of working together. Let all involved work together for all involved. Allow solutions to be tested through the framework of partnership, rightness, and contribution. Let every offended voice and victim bring an offering of solutions to the table, along with those who convene these conversations. It is time to disempower a federal response and activate a local response. Let every community test and approve the perfect will of God in their situation. Let no celebration occur until people have painstakingly completed the work ahead.

It could be that the church becomes the most sensible voice with the most influence in the conversation of discrimination. We are battling for the hearts and souls of human beings. This is more than just casting a ballot or pushing through legislation. Laws are lazy things unless people empower them through action. Laws can never care, cry, or hug. Laws cannot touch or hold. They cannot empathize. Laws do not make people better; people make people better. This may be a divine moment in time where divine destiny grabs hold of a painful issue. What is needed is the manifestation of God's power into the communities that are victimized and struggling with a prejudicial reality.

Early last summer, our community was faced with a divisive issue that made national headlines. The issue settled around the question of force used by a white police officer against a group of African-American students at a swimming pool party. Because the neighborhood involved was in a more affluent area, the media began with their

immediate bias of white, wealthy residents against young
African-Americans. Most of the media stories were pre-
written fabrications to match previous racism stories par-
alleling Ferguson, Missouri, and Baltimore, Maryland.
But the story in McKinney, Texas, was different, in part
because of what happened behind the event.

I am thankful to be part of a group of ministers in
our community; we refer to our group as the McKinney
Shepherds. For the last four years, we have met once a
month to connect, encourage, and build up one another.
We do our best to care for one another and meet together
socially. We are a mixed group of different theological
persuasions, denominations, experience, race, ethnicities,
and various church sizes. Our common interest is that we
live and pastor together in the same city. We don't com-
pete with each other; we serve one another.

A few months after the riots in Ferguson, Missouri, we
asked ourselves this question during our monthly meeting:
"What would we do if McKinney experienced a Ferguson
incident?" As we began to discuss our response, little
did we know that in less than eight weeks we would be
faced with a national news story of an unrestrained police
response to African-American teenagers. Honestly, video
clips released to the media of the incident were framing an
inaccurate picture of our city and our citizens.

I still remember the Sunday afternoon before the story
broke. A prayer warrior in my church called me and said,
"You need to get ready because in less than twenty-four
hours, McKinney, Texas, will be in the national news over
allegations of discrimination, racism, and police force." I
was stunned. I asked this prayer warrior how could this
be, and her response was that something had happened
the afternoon before that would unleash the press upon

the city. Her comment to me was that "the pastors of our city need to get ahead of this; if not, it could get really bad."

I grabbed my cell phone and called three other pastors in our group. As I called and explained to these pastors the situation, one reached out to the mayor and police chief for an "all clergy, only clergy" meeting the next day. Another reached out to the African-American and Hispanic pastors in our group and city. By 10:30 p.m. on that Sunday night, a large majority of the pastors and clergy had been contacted and organized to meet the next evening.

On Monday evening, more than one hundred community pastors and clergy gathered in an undisclosed location to privately meet with the mayor and newly appointed police chief. We discussed the events of what appeared to be an excessive police response to African-American teens. The meeting was extremely respectful, honorable, and sincere.

The meeting began. Only one news reporter was permitted to attend, and that was only for the first hour. While the meeting was occurring, the Black Panthers were organizing a march, and other civil rights protesters were arriving by bus. By the end of the evening, almost one thousand demonstrators had arrived to protest our sleepy, suburban community. Stories of overt racism, prejudice, and discrimination filled the news channels. But in our meeting with the clergy and city pastors, God was writing a different story.

Minority-based congregations were represented by their pastors. These pastors shared openly and honestly about the feelings and incidences of perceived racism and discrimination in our city. They shared experiences where they felt their needs were neglected or ignored by our community leaders. They were transparent and kind. Not once did they express disrespect or anger toward our city leaders, police, or community leaders. But they did express their concerns and the issues associated with "white blindness." I had pastored in our city for more than twelve years and never realized some of the issues these minority pastors dealt with in their community. For many of us Anglo pastors, our hearts were stirred and moved by the words spoken that evening.

As these pastors spoke, others shared as well. These were voices of wisdom, grace, forgiveness, and empathy. Although each of us pastored different congregations in different sections of our city, our concern was for the city. We could not allow the national media to write a fictional tale to fit a national story line. We could not allow the Black Panthers and other militant groups to stir hatred and animosity amidst a community that lived together and cared for one another. While activists were flying in and arriving by the hour, the pastors and clergy of our city had determined that the outside forces of activism would not destroy our community.

African-American pastors pledged to gather their people for prayer, works of compassion, and exhortations of restraint. Hispanic pastors pledged their support and directed their community through strategic responses. Anglo pastors pledged honesty, understanding, and support to the minority communities, as well as to hold the city leaders accountable for their actions. What should have been a meeting of division turned out to be a gathering of unity. We had determined as clergy and pastors that our city would not burn; there would not be riots, violence, civil disobedience, disorder, destruction, or harm. Then we prayed.

All the clergy and every pastor present gathered around our mayor and police chief and laid hands on them in prayer. We prayed and repented for the sins of discrimination and racism that occurred in our community, left unnoticed and unaddressed. We prayed against destructive spiritual influences, demonic spirits, private agendas, hurt feelings, media misrepresentations, division, violence, and people who would do harm to our city and citizens. In prayer, we loosed upon our community, its leaders, and representatives the Spirit of God, the peace of God, the wisdom of God, and the protection of the Lord. We called forth a spirit of unity, compassion, and understanding. We made spiritual history in our city that Monday night.

The agitators left our city within five days because they could not get enough angry people to protest. What could have been a national news story lasting for weeks turned out to be a blip on a five-day news cycle because the church decided to come together, work together to preserve our community, and address our own problems and issues. We avoided what should have been a civic explosion because God led pastors by His Spirit and we responded in wisdom.

From that evening forward, we have met together as a combined group of spiritual leaders. We have shared blessings, preached in each other's churches, and carried each other's burdens. We have not been perfect in all that we have done, but we have been together. We have more work to do as spiritual leaders and contemporaries, but the city leaders know the pastors are united together. We are leading the citizens of our city in steps of faith, grace, compassion, mercy, and transformation.

There is a need for the church to take the lead in these community issues. This is not a place for arrogance, but for humbleness. It is not a call for a community reaction, but for community revival. It is not a place for media sound-bites, but for ministry and compassion.

Honestly, in our community, the African-American pastors decided how their community would respond, and they led them in that response. Their community followed the examples of their spiritual leaders. Discrimination is a culturally relevant subject, waiting to be addressed by the church. Speaking as a spiritual voice and leading people toward community transformation is the role of the church. We must lead by example and not by rhetoric.

The true answer to the disparities in our country will not be found at the voting booth, in a politician, or in a political party. The true answer to these issues is found in the living God and His Son, Jesus Christ. God holds the world together, and the name of Jesus is the highest name or word that can be spoken by human lips. Jesus removes all disparities.

Jesus is not just the cure; He is the cause! It's in the name of Jesus that prejudice, bigotry, discrimination, and racism find their silence. Jesus is the answer for humanity, and the church has been authorized to declare Him as the answer to America and the nations. It's time for Christ-followers and the church to pull down the strongholds of discrimination. It's time to heal and transform the leper on the road.

Chapter 8

KINGDOM BUILDING

The Political Doctrine of Jesus

G ALATIANS 4:4 STATES, "When the right time came, God sent his Son." This verse means *exactly* what it says: Jesus came to the earth at the right time. Have you ever had a "right on time" experience? You know the feeling—when time and timing work together for something similar to the miraculous. There is something about being "in time and on time" that boosts our confidence and reminds us that someone bigger than ourselves is working for our good. *Time is when the season is right, and timing is when the moment is right.*

Everything in the life of Christ came down to seasons and moments. Jesus used seasons and moments to work simultaneously for His purpose. When the season did not correspond to the moment, Jesus either changed the season or withdrew from the moment.

TRAITS OF TIMING

Divine timing creates a life rhythm. Jesus functioned in divine rhythm. He emphasized time and timing when He said, "My time has not come." At one point, in John 7:1–9, He even told His brother, "Now is not the right time for me to go, but you can go anytime." Then in Mark 14:41 and Luke 21:8, Jesus stated, "The time has come." Divine rhythm directed Jesus. What appears to be coincidental with Jesus was actually seasons and moments in rhythm.

Divine timing influences the harvest of souls. Another way Jesus viewed time and timing was in relation to the harvest of souls. In John 4:35, Jesus said, "You know the saying, 'Four months between planting and harvest.' But I say, wake up and look around. The fields are already ripe for harvest." Jesus was keenly aware of time and timing. He understood the spiritual seasons and moments as they related to the harvest of souls.

Divine timing is always tested. In John 8:1–11, an adulterous woman was thrown before the feet of Jesus. The religious leaders knew where to find this woman and when to get her in order to test Jesus. When she was cast down at His feet, Jesus responded by writing in the sand. Jesus was inserting a "divine pause" into a very tense moment of judgment. Jesus handled divine timing so well; the opportunity to judge and execute this woman passed by, and her life was spared. She was given a new opportunity to live free from condemnation.

Divine timing is the outflow of obedience. In John 4:4, Jesus had to go through Samaria. It was customary that when Jewish people traveled north from Jerusalem toward Galilee, they would first journey east, cross over the Jordan River, and then go north. In doing so, they would avoid the despicable residents of Samaria. Samaritans had a corrupted Jewish bloodline, so they were despised by pure-blooded Jews.

Jesus showed up at the well of Jacob at noon, only to be greeted by a woman who had been in five marriages and was currently involved with another lover. She was amazed Jesus would speak to her and drink from her water jug. Jesus was right on time for her late midday appearance. His arrival was the key to her survival. Her life turned around because of timing. She was the reason Jesus was there.

Divine timing released the miraculous. There are so many timing instances recorded in the Gospels that are so precise, they simply could not be coincidence. These instances seem miraculous in themselves. Look at the events of Luke 7:11–15. The widow of Nain is burying her son as Jesus walked into her town. Jesus touched the coffin and raised the young man from the dead. If Jesus had arrived 30 minutes later, the man would have been buried.

Divine timing works through tension. Jesus was familiar with the tension of time and timing. In John 11, Jesus allowed his good friend Lazarus to die when Jesus was only a forty-minute walk from his house. Then Jesus waited four days to visit his grieving friends. Jesus ignored their call to come and heal Lazarus. Jesus ignored the wake and funeral. Then four days later, Jesus visited a grief-stricken family, purposed to raise Lazarus from the dead.

Often, the Scriptures reveal that Jesus pushed through time to arrive at timing. The very first miracle Jesus performed was at the wedding in Cana of Galilee in John 2:1–10. People marvel that Jesus turned water into wine. But the real miracle was that Jesus pushed through time to arrive at timing.

In John 2:4, Jesus told His mother, who insisted He help the bridal party in their wine crisis, "My hour has not yet come." Jesus was not ready to move into the ministry of miracles. Jesus knew that once He opened this realm publicly, there would be no closing it while He walked the Earth. Yet His response was not sufficient for His mother. She turned and ignored Jesus. She addressed the servants instead, saying, "Whatever He says to you, do it!"

Jesus simply commanded stone water pots be filled with water and then a cup be drawn and given to the master of the feast. In those few moments between being drawn to being drunk, water became wine. Jesus pushed through time and arrived at timing.

In another instance, look at the response of Jesus to the woman from Canaan in Matthew 15:21–28 (NKJV):

> Then Jesus went out from there and departed to the region of Tyre and Sidon. And behold, a woman of Canaan came from that region and cried out to Him, saying, "Have mercy on me, O Lord, Son of David! My daughter is severely demon-possessed." But He answered her not a word. And His disciples came and urged Him, saying, "Send her away, for she cries out after us." But He answered and said, "I was not sent except to the lost sheep of the house of Israel."
>
> Then she came and worshiped Him, saying, "Lord, help me!" But He answered and said, "It is not good to take the children's bread and throw it to the little dogs." And she said, "Yes, Lord, yet even the little dogs eat the crumbs which fall from their masters' table." Then Jesus answered and said to her, "O woman, great is your faith! Let it be to you as you desire." And her daughter was healed from that very hour."

Jesus did everything He could do to protect His season of manifestation. Jesus was sent to the Jewish people first. He did not want to violate the divine order of His manifestation. Jesus ultimately knew this woman's daughter would be set free from demonic possession; that's the reason Jesus came to the earth! But He did not want to push through time until He could finish revealing Himself to the Jews.

What did Jesus do to protect His season? First, He ignored the woman; then He insulted her and called her a little dog. But this woman was tenacious for her miracle. Her response was simply, "I'm not asking for the loaf of bread, just a crumb!" Her response got to Jesus. This woman exercised the same faith Jesus's mother had in John 2. What was His response? His response was to push through time and move into timing. Jesus passed up the season to get into the moment!

Divine timing is motion sensitive. As Jesus pushed through time to arrive at timing, He also proved that the kingdom of God exists in continual motion. Galatians 5:25 states that we are to keep in step with the Spirit. The kingdom of God works on the dynamic of timing as much as it does faith. However, the kingdom of God is manifested through the domain of peace, righteousness and joy (Romans 14:17). This part of the kingdom exists above the fray of spiritual warfare. The kingdom of God is in continual motion and movement. It is an active realm with no interference or interruption. Motion is attached to this kingdom; therefore, time is in constant motion.

> It was in the midst of the ordinary that Jesus extracted the extraordinary.

Time is the incubator of divine timing. It was in the midst of the ordinary that Jesus extracted the extraordinary. When everything looked natural, Jesus did something supernatural. It was within this framework that Jesus declared something new over people. He spoke with declarative tones the principles and precepts that brought new truths into existence. He was relentless. He chose the time and the timing to declare hope over those who were burdened and to bring understanding to those bound by confusion. Something new was being born across the Earth. In the fullness of time, timing was giving birth to the manifested, organic presence of its Creator. Dual, parallel kingdoms were about to be revealed to humankind, and divine timing was the instigator of their inception.

TWO PARALLEL KINGDOMS

Just as Jesus came to earth fully man and fully God, He taught about the existence of two kingdoms. The first was the kingdom of God, and the second was the kingdom of heaven. Many people believe that these are synonymous kingdoms presented in Scripture with a generalized concept. Although these kingdoms do intermingle at times and have been used interchangeably, there are some specific instances where they are completely separated and refer to two very different realms.

I define the kingdom of God as the domain/realm of the Spirit of God and the kingdom of heaven as the domain/realm of the saint. The phrase "kingdom of God" is used five times in the Gospel of Matthew and fifty-four times in the Gospels. It should be noted that only Matthew uses both terms—*kingdom of God* and *kingdom of heaven,* while the other three Gospel writers refer only to the kingdom of God. Honestly, Matthew uses the term *kingdom of God* in matters that relate specifically to the Holy Spirit. The major difference is the kingdom of God refers to the *rule* of God whereas the kingdom of heaven refers to the *realm* of the believer.

In my view, Matthew appears to be the most reliable source for details within the Gospels. Matthew writes analytically and with specificity. There are a few occasions in which both Matthew and Luke share the same information, but the order is different. A great example of this can be found in the temptations of Jesus in Matthew 4 and Luke 4. Both writers agree on the temptations of Christ, but list them in a different order. Because Matthew was a direct follower and a disciple, whereas Luke was a follower of Christ but also maintained his physician practice, it would seem the former tax collector turned disciple would be the most reliable source for details. Matthew is a detail guy!

THE KINGDOM OF GOD

It seems Matthew was intrigued by these dual realms. He is the only Gospel writer to record both terms. His first mention of the kingdom of God is in Matthew 6:33: "But seek first the kingdom of God and His righteousness, and all these things shall be added to you." The word *kingdom* is translated from the Greek word *basileia,* and it is properly translated "royalty," that is, (abstractly) *"rule"* or (concretely) a "realm." It means literally a kingdom, or figuratively to reign.[1] So we understand that anytime the word *kingdom* appears in the teachings of Jesus, Jesus is discussing a realm and not a location. The word *God* comes from the Greek word *theos. Theos* means a deity, especially the supreme divinity.[2] This is where we get our word *theo* as in theology or the study of God.

In Matthew 12:24–33, the Pharisees accused Jesus of being full of demonic power because He cast demons out of people. When this accusation was leveled, Jesus responded with a very confrontational tone.

> Now when the Pharisees heard it they said, "This fellow does not cast out demons except by Beelzebub, the ruler of the demons." But Jesus knew their thoughts, and said to them: "Every kingdom divided against itself is brought to desolation, and every city or house divided against itself will not stand. If Satan casts out Satan, he is divided against himself. How then will his kingdom stand? And if I cast out demons by Beelzebub, by whom do your sons cast them out? Therefore, they shall be your judges. But if I cast out demons by the Spirit of God,

surely the kingdom of God has come upon you. Or how can one enter a strong man's house and plunder his goods, unless he first binds the strong man? And then he will plunder his house. He who is not with Me is against Me, and he who does not gather with Me scatters abroad.

Therefore I say to you, every sin and blasphemy will be forgiven men, but the blasphemy against the Spirit will not be forgiven men. Anyone who speaks a word against the Son of Man, it will be forgiven him; but whoever speaks against the Holy Spirit, it will not be forgiven him, either in this age or in the age to come."

The kingdom of God is the realm and domain of the Holy Spirit. Jesus was very clear when He said, "If I cast out demons by the Spirit of God, surely the kingdom of God has come upon you." When Jesus operated in the casting out of demons, He operated in the realm of the Holy Spirit, which is the kingdom of God.

The context of this truth is in the next few verses. Jesus scolded the Pharisees for blaspheming the Holy Spirit. He made it clear that when they attribute the work of the Holy Spirit to Satan, it constitutes blasphemy and will not be forgiven. Jesus was very deliberate and protective over the realm of the Holy Spirit. The context of this passage confirmed that the kingdom of God is the realm and domain of the Spirit.

The next passage is Matthew 19:23–24. Here Jesus has spoken with the rich young ruler, who left the conversation with Jesus quite discouraged because of his attachment to wealth. "Then Jesus said to His disciples, 'Assuredly, I say to you that it is hard for a rich man to enter the kingdom of heaven. And again I say to you, it is easier for a camel to go through the eye of a needle than for a rich man to enter the kingdom of God.'" Notice that Jesus mentioned both domains—the domain of heaven and the domain of God.

In this passage, Jesus highlighted that trusting in worldly possessions creates an enormous difficulty in flowing in the realm of saint and in the realm of the Spirit. The man's wealth was not the issue; rather, the man's love and trust in wealth was the issue. His wealth got in the way of his obedience.

The realm of atoning faith and the realm of Spirit power require a trust in God that supersedes our ability to provide and care for ourselves. Should we provide and care for ourselves? Absolutely. But in our desire to provide and care for ourselves, we cannot depend on our efforts or love our successes more than we trust and follow Jesus. The issue in this passage is not wealth; it is heart.

The kingdom of heaven and the kingdom of God require submission of the heart. Everything has to belong to God and be given over to God to function in these realms. Jesus noted that self-trust and disobedience created barriers to the domain of the saint and the domain of the Spirit. Jesus was very direct and deliberate. We can attach ourselves to things on the earth that block or impede our ability to function in the domain of the saint and the domain of the Spirit.

Another way to understand this is the way Jesus illustrated these two kingdoms. Referring to the kingdom of heaven, He said that it was "hard," meaning it was impractical or fastidious. Notice Jesus did not say that it was impossible; rather, that it was not practical. It was impractical for people who trust completely in their wealth to trust completely in Christ. Then Jesus said it is easier for a camel to enter through the eye of the needle. Understanding this statement requires a little knowledge of a biblical anecdote.

Tradition holds that there was a "needle" gate near or in

the wall built around Jerusalem. It was used as a night gate as well as for large animals to enter through. The animal,— or, in this instance, the camel—had to be stripped of its saddles and packs in order to crawl on its knees through the entrance. It was a difficult, arduous task.

Whether this gate was factual or hyperbole, the truth Jesus is emphasizing is that it is difficult for people who trust in wealth to enter into the realm of God's Spirit. This realm of the Spirit requires a humbling and emptying of ourselves. Again, this is not about money or wealth, but it is about dependency, trust, and faith in God. Operating in the realm of the kingdom of God requires much more submission and transparency than the kingdom of heaven.

In Matthew 21:31–32, Jesus expounds on this matter: "Jesus said to them, 'Assuredly, I say to you that tax collectors and harlots enter the kingdom of God before you. For John came to you in the way of righteousness, and you did not believe him; but tax collectors and harlots believed him; and when you saw it, you did not afterward relent and believe him.'"

Jesus hammers the chief priests and spiritual elders for their unbelief and for challenging Jesus's authority and teachings. Jesus makes it clear that the harlots and tax collectors, the real sinners of their culture, were entering the domain of the Spirit ahead of the religious teachers. They were entering through faith, transparency, and submission through belief in John's message about Jesus. While the religious teachers were seeking out knowledge, these former sinners were seeking out the Spirit!

The implication is that entering the domain of the saint, which is the kingdom of heaven, is done by faith. Once that realm has been entered, the domain of the Spirit which is the kingdom of God is next. Everything in these realms pivots on faith!

Let's look at one last scripture in Matthew 21:42-43.

> Jesus said to them, "Have you never read in the
> Scriptures: 'The stone which the builders rejected
> has become the chief cornerstone. This was the
> LORD's doing, and it is marvelous in our eyes'?
> Therefore I say to you, the kingdom of God will be
> taken from you and given to a nation bearing the
> fruits of it."

Again, Jesus is very intentional in His statement. Since
they have rejected Jesus as the chief cornerstone, the
domain of the Spirit which is the kingdom of God will be
taken from them and given to a different nation bearing
the fruits of it. In the Jewish mindset and culture, they
were the only people or nation who could receive divine
revelation and power. Jesus speaks clearly to them and
confirms that if they reject the Cornerstone, they reject
the kingdom of God, the realm of the Spirit.

Notice the reference of fruits attached to the kingdom of
God in this passage. Jesus declared that not only will the
essence of the Holy Spirit's person and power be removed
from them, but the fruit of these things will be removed.
They were losing future fruit by rejecting Christ.

God is the one who raises up nations and kings. In
rejecting Jesus, the Jewish people went to the back of the
line. From that moment on, generations of Jews would be
raised up and perish across the earth without the fruitfulness of the kingdom of God in their lives. This may be the
reason why many Jews still reject Jesus as their Savior. Their
hearts are hard from the absence of God's Spirit moving
within them. They have rejected the kingdom of God.

Beyond the fruitfulness of the Spirit is His dominion.
The dominion of the Holy Spirit is shown in Scripture as
the sevenfold Spirit of God (Rev 1:4; 3:1). We know there

is only one Spirit according to 1 Corinthians 12:4–6 and Ephesians 2:18; 4:4. Yet, the number seven ascribed to the Spirit is used to communicate the wholeness or completeness of God's Spirit. Isaiah 11:2 reveals the meaning of the sevenfold Spirit, or as some translations read, the Seven Spirits of God.

> The Spirit of the Lord shall rest upon Him, the Spirit of wisdom and understanding, the Spirit of counsel and might, the Spirit of knowledge and of the fear of the Lord.

Let's look briefly at each of these titles describing the Holy Spirit. Each title describes a facet of the kingdom of God given to believers through the Holy Spirit.

The Spirit of the Lord. This refers to the self-existent attribute of the Spirit. He is not dependent on someone or something else to exist. He is His own force, energy, life, and being.

The Spirit of wisdom. The Spirit is the ultimate source of wisdom. The Bible states that God made the world with wisdom through faith (Prov. 3:19; Heb. 11:3). James 4:17 teaches that there is a Spirit-sourced wisdom that comes from heaven. This is the Spirit of wisdom contained within the Holy Spirit.

The Spirit of understanding. This is the Spirit's ability to see, know, and distinguish beyond what is seen and known. The root word for *understanding* in the Hebrew language means to separate mentally and distinguish. Often in the Scriptures, wisdom and understanding are linked or mentioned together. Understanding is the flip side of wisdom.

The Spirit of counsel. This is more than just good advice; it is providing counsel that contains the most prudent solutions with resolve. Counsel is always the right advice.

Jesus stated that the Spirit would counsel believers. We should expect the best counsel and advice from the Spirit.

The Spirit of might. This refers to the force and power that resides within the Spirit. The Spirit of God contains the absolute strength, force, and might of God. His might is so strong that it raised Christ from the dead (Rom. 8:11).

The Spirit of knowledge. This is the ability to know and to be aware. The Spirit functions in this capacity according to 1 Corinthians 2:10–12. The Spirit searches the deep things of God in order to convey those things to us so we can know them. The realm of Spirit knowledge is more than facts or data; it is the ability to make us aware and to reveal what needs to be known.

The Spirit of the fear of the Lord. This is manifestation of reverence and respect. It is a healthy fear displayed toward authority. It is the atmosphere of worship, adoration, and moral reverence.

The Holy Spirit exercises dominion in these realms because the kingdom of God is a realm of authority. There is no warfare present in the kingdom of God; there is no rebellion, chaos, or principality. There is peace, dominion, reverence, and fear in the kingdom of God.

THE KINGDOM OF HEAVEN

Just as the kingdom of God is a realm of authority and the domain of the Spirit, the kingdom of heaven is a realm of anointing and the domain of the saint. The major differences between these realms are their purpose and realm of rule. All believers are saints, and the saints of God are anointed for warfare and victory.

As Christ-followers, our purpose is to do spiritual battle on this earth, to cast down imaginations and pull down strongholds (2 Cor. 10:3–5). We have received an anointing from the Holy One to receive revelation and instruction in this life (1 John 2:20, 27). Through Christ, we are led in triumphant procession (2 Cor. 2:14). We are called to this realm to exercise the authority of Christ. We are equipped and released for spiritual battle (Eph. 6:10–18). This is the realm of the saint's dominion!

The kingdom of heaven is the dominion of holy saints. That's what Christians, Christ-followers, and believers are called; 1 Corinthians 1:2 calls us saints! Matthew 16:19 states the believer has been given the keys to the kingdom of heaven. As Christ-followers, we have the ability to bind and loosen, to agree and claim. We are released into this realm to prevail against the gates of hell. Matthew 17:20 states that when we operate in this realm through faith, nothing will be impossible, as we believe in God!

The kingdom of heaven is mentioned thirty-one times in Matthew. This is the realm of warfare and battle. This phrase is mentioned often because it's the realm believers dwell in. It's the place of spiritual confrontation and confiscation. It is the realm where Christ-followers claim souls and battle on behalf of people. There is no room for confusion or laziness in this realm. It is the realm of spiritual possession and uprising. The kingdom of heaven is the place where anointings are released and victories are won.

Jesus taught this kingdom suffers violently while advancing, and it is violently apprehended (Matt. 11:12). The presence of Jesus on the earth was proof positive that this eternal battle over humanity was very personal to God. Timing was key in this fight. There is often great spiritual violence and warfare that surrounds the manifestation of the kingdom of heaven.

There are some peculiar advantages saints have in this realm. Let's look at those advantages.

1) Saints have been given the mysteries of the kingdom of heaven (Matt. 13:11). The Holy Spirit has anointed

Christ-followers to know the secrets and hidden truths of Christ. Christ formed the world, and His secrets and truths are embedded in creation. Jesus is the Word, the Eternal Word, and the vibrations of His voice still rock the planetary substance of space. Jesus was and is the mystery of God, hidden from the rulers of the age (2 Cor. 2:8). What the saints have been given is truly the mystery of the Messiah, or what the Apostle Paul calls in Colossians 1:27, "Christ in you." Jesus is not only the mystery of the kingdom of heaven, but He is the biggest part of it!

2) Saints have been given the keys of the kingdom of heaven (Matt. 16:19). As believers, we have been given the authority, (the keys) to literally lock out the demonic and the satanic. We have been given authority to reduce the geographical domain and spiritual influence of the enemy. Jesus left His body of believers as kingdom stewards on this Earth. We are to dominate this realm. What great authority the body of Christ has been vested with that we should rule in this life through Christ (Rom. 5:17). To do anything less would be to vacate the very authority delegated to us as believers. As saints, we need to open what needs to be opened and close what needs to be closed!

3) We are called to model and reproduce the principles of the kingdom of heaven (Matt. 5:19). These are reproducible principles and concepts. There is something simple about the domain of the saint that is easy to reproduce through example. Kingdom laws and principles are inspirational, and they lift the human spirit into avowed excellence. People crave the victorious atmosphere associated with the kingdom of heaven. This is why we are to reproduce it continually.

4) We enter the kingdom of heaven by doing the will of the Father (Matt. 7:21). Nothing beats obedience; it's the main currency of the kingdom of heaven. Following the

Father's will is the crux of the kingdom. Living in obedience positions us for favor, victory, and the release of miraculous.

5) *The kingdom of heaven is to be preached with authority and results (Matt. 10:7).* Every time Jesus sent the disciples out to minister, supernatural results were experienced. Preaching Jesus is preaching the kingdom of heaven.

The kingdom of heaven is your incubator to destiny and greatness.

---

6) *The kingdom of heaven is an incubator of greatness (Matt. 11:11).* Jesus said the least in the kingdom of heaven is greater than John the Baptist. John was the forerunner of Christ. Jesus could not appear until John appeared. John released a message that caused people to hunger for the Messiah. Yet, in the kingdom of heaven, the least is greater than John.

The kingdom of heaven is your incubator to destiny and greatness. Your past does not matter, only the kingdom of heaven matters. Transformation is the process of this kingdom. God's greatness in you is real, it's powerful, and it's transforming! Receive this promise! God wants you to be renowned in His presence.

7) *The kingdom of heaven is multi-faceted (Matt. 13).* Jesus teaches seven dynamic principles about the kingdom of God in this chapter. Look at these principles.

The kingdom of heaven is:

- *Individual.* Every person receives the same gospel, but everyone does something different with it (Matt. 13:18–23).

- *Indestructible.* Even though the enemy sows false seed and hypocrisy into the kingdom, he cannot destroy it (Matt. 13:24–30).

- *Influential.* Just a little dose of the kingdom message can work through the human heart and transform everyone who receives it (Matt. 13:33–34).

- *Inventoried.* Everyone in the kingdom of heaven will give an account to God (Matt. 13:36–43).

- *Investment.* We give all we can and sell what we possess to move the kingdom of heaven forward. Nothing on earth is worth more than the kingdom of heaven (Matt. 13:44–46).

- *Inspected.* The wicked will be removed from the just in the kingdom of heaven (Matt. 13:47–50).

- *Informative.* The kingdom of heaven releases new revelation and old truths into the lives of people; the Word is informative (Matt. 13:50–52).

8) The kingdom of heaven is comprised of children (Matt. 19:14). There is no one who knows, loves, and blesses children like Jesus. The Holy Spirit fellowships with children in the womb (Ps. 139:13–16). It is natural for children to believe in God because they have been exposed to Him in the creative process. Children believe more than they know; they possess greater faith even though they possess less knowledge. This is how we should be in the kingdom of heaven.

9) The kingdom of heaven is the place of justice (Matt. 20:1). God is not into fairness; He is into justice. Fairness deals with equality, but justice deals with rightness. God is right and righteous in all things. People can petition the kingdom of heaven for justice, and God will deliver it.

10) *The kingdom of heaven is a place that accepts everyone (Matt. 22:2).* Jesus died for every person, so the kingdom of heaven is made for everyone. Social standing has no standing in this kingdom. This kingdom is comprised of all races, tribes, and nations. Rich or poor, healthy or sick, free or slave, man or woman—it does not matter. What matters is that people accept forgiveness through Jesus. He is the door to this kingdom.

11) *The kingdom of heaven operates through wisdom (Matt. 25:2).* Wisdom is the principal thing (Prov. 4:7). Wisdom is a core value and a prevailing principle in the kingdom of heaven. This realm leverages things seen and unseen, tangible and intangible, things of earth and above the earth in order to gain souls. Wisdom is strategic and valued.

12) *The kingdom of heaven requires multiplication stewardship (Matt. 25:14).* Everything of God multiplies. Multiplication is the mentality of God because fullness is His nature. There is no lack in the kingdom of heaven because God multiplies everything within the kingdom against itself. Even the death of a saint produces life from the multiplied presence of the Savior within that person! The best way to experience the kingdom is to do so through multiplication!

13) *The kingdom of heaven is a realm of warfare (Eph. 6:11–12).* This is a realm of spiritual battle. The kingdom of heaven is violent; that is how Jesus described it in Matthew 11:12. This is no place for the coward or the worrier. The kingdom of heaven has been passed through the blood-stained corridors of time. It is a place where people commit their life and some give their life to see the kingdom of heaven flourish.

This is a kingdom that places a demand on faithfulness, commitment, sacrifice, obedience, and courage. Spiritual warfare is the most difficult warfare of all. The kingdom of heaven is on the front edge of spiritual conquest! This is why this kingdom requires spiritual armor, spiritual gifts, spiritual knowledge, spiritual fruit, praying in the Spirit, and the Word of God. Our assignment is to battle, defeat, and lock Satan out of this realm!

14) There are three core values in the kingdom of heaven:

- Repentance. This is its message (Matt. 4:17).

- Obedience. This is its mandate (Matt. 7:21).

- Apprehension. This is its mantle (Matt. 11:12).

As Christians we live in both realms of the kingdom. We exist in the spiritual dominion of the Spirit while we battle in the spiritual dimension of the saint. Just as Jesus was both fully human and fully God, as Christ-followers we are fully engaged in the realm of the Holy Spirit and the realm of our confession of faith. This is why we are anointed and given authority.

We battle for spiritual ground, holding onto what we have gained. There is no armor for the backside of the believer; all the spiritual armor is offensive. We are born again for spiritual battles and spiritually designed to dominate in the name of Jesus! We are kingdom people and kingdom citizens! These realms belong to us, and the glory belongs to Christ!

Chapter 9

THOSE NOT WITH US

J ESUS WAS 100 percent truth and 100 percent grace. Compassion was the very center of His existence. Jesus truly was an artisan of grace.

> Now it came to pass, when the time had come for Him to be received up, that He steadfastly set His face to go to Jerusalem, and sent messengers before His face. And as they went, they entered a village of the Samaritans, to prepare for Him. But they did not receive Him, because His face was set for the journey to Jerusalem. And when His disciples James and John saw this, they said, "Lord, do You want us to command fire to come down from heaven and consume them, just as Elijah did?" But He turned and rebuked them, and said, "You do not know what manner of spirit you are of. For the Son of Man did not come to destroy men's lives but to save them." And they went to another village.
> —LUKE 9:51–56

The disciples loved showing off Christ's power and authority when they dealt with people they did not like. The Samaritans were despised by the disciples. The disciples believed releasing supernatural consuming fire against those who rejected Christ was the right response to unbelief. Jesus rebuked the short-sightedness of the disciples and reminded them that they were to be of a different spirit. He did not come to destroy people, but to save them!

American politics has changed and the political tension in the twenty-first century has only gotten worse. There is little hope politics will ever return to civility and decency. The media, social media, and a twenty-four-hour news cycle only embeds into society the acrimony of broken political promises, partisan politics, and the ever-widening divide of governmental philosophies and ideologies.

However, as Christ-followers, we are instructed to be different. To quote Jesus in Luke 9:55, "You do not know what manner of spirit you are of!" People will not find the Jesus who came to save them when we are using the gospel to destroy them.

We are called to the generations we live with.

So as this book comes to an end, here are five statements and five questions to think about and answer. These statements deserve full consideration. Perhaps in the space provided, you may want to think through these statements and write how you will present the politics of Jesus.

1. Christians need to find ways to reconnect with the culture, so they can influence it and not antagonize it. How are you going to reconnect with the culture?

---

2. The American culture needs to be reintro-
   duced to the *message* of Jesus Christ—not
   doctrine, denominations, or political affilia-
   tions. How are you going to reintroduce the
   message of Jesus?

   _____

   _____

   _____

3. The twelve disciples prove a Christ-follower
   does not have to change political ideologies
   or parties to be truly saved by the grace of
   Jesus Christ. How are you going to embrace
   other Christ-followers who have different or
   perhaps opposite political ideologies?

   _____

   _____

   _____

4. The kingdom of heaven and the kingdom of
   God require our full engagement as Christ-
   followers. How are you going to engage in the
   realm of the saint and the realm of the Spirit?

   _____

   _____

   _____

5. Social issues cannot divide the body of
   Christ because a fractured church cannot
   heal or mend a fractured society. How are
   you going to biblically respond to social
   issues to build unity in the body of Christ?

_____

_____

_____

We are called to the generations we live with. God has destined us for this time in history. As Christ-followers, our message is greater than our differences. May God empower you through the Spirit to manifest the message of Christ with clarity, compassion, and grace. Now it's your time to go and make a difference in our culture and in our nation. May God be with you, direct you and grant you great success as you bestow the kingdom of God and heaven upon others. After all, the politics of Jesus is best stated by Jesus Himself in Matthew 6:10: "Thy kingdom come, thy will be done, on earth as it is in heaven."

NOTES

CHAPTER 1: A DOSE OF PERSPECTIVE

1. Ravi Zacharias, Synergize Conference, Orlando, FL, 23 January 2016.
2. Ken Rudin, "Everyone under Pressure in Rangel Case," *Political Junkie,* http://www.npr.org/sections/politicaljunkie/2010/07/29/128856206/everyone-under-pressure-in-rangel-case, 29 July 2010, accessed 25 July 2016.

CHAPTER 4: SAMARIA IS CALLING

1. N. Z. Edward and Stanford University (eds), *Stanford Encyclopedia of Philosophy: By the Metaphysics Research Lab* (Stanford, CA: Stanford University Press, 2004).
2. "Identity Politics," *Rational Wiki* (2015), http://rationalwiki.org/wiki/Identity_politics, accessed 25 July 2016.
3. Margaret Mowszko, "A Brief History of the Samaritans," *New Life,* http://newlife.id.au/a-brief-history-of-the-samaritans/, September 2009; accessed 25 July 2016.
4. Ibid.

CHAPTER 6: I DO

1. Jeffrey Rosen, "The Dangers of a Constitutional 'Right to Dignity,'" *The Atlantic,* 29 April 2015, http://www.theatlantic.com/politics/archive/2015/04/the-dangerous-doctrine-of-dignity/391796/, accessed 25 July 2016.
2. Jim Kennedy, "What the Professional Organizations Say," 6 December 2004, http://teachthefacts.org/resources-professionalorgs.html, accessed 25 July 2016.
3. Ed Young, "No, Scientists Have Not Found the 'Gay Gene,'" *The Atlantic Periodical,* 20 October 2015, http://www.theatlantic.com/science/archive/2015/10/no-scientists-have-not-found-the-gay-gene/410059/, accessed 25 July 2016.
4. Selwyn Duke, "Shocking Times: Movement for Pedophile "Rights" Marches On," *The New American,* http://www.thenewamerican.com/culture/item/21664-shocking- times-movement-for-pedophile-rights-marches-on, 28 September 2015, accessed 25 July 2016.
5. Kurt Nimmo, "Gays Rights May Open Door for Pedophile Rights," *InfoWars,* 2 July 2015, http://www.infowars.com/

gays-rights-may-open-door-for-pedophile-rights/, accessed 25 July 2015.

6. "Abomination"/*tô'êbah,* Strong's #8441, http://www.studylight. org/lexicons/hebrew/hwview.cgi?n=8441, accessed 25 July 2016.

7. "Perversion"/*tebel,* Strong's #8397, http://www.studylight.org/ lexicons/hebrew/hwview.cgi?n=8397, accessed 25 July 2016.

8. Susan Schoenian, "Sheep 201," 7 November 2015, http://www. sheep101.info/201/about.html, accessed 25 July 2016.

CHAPTER 7: THE LEPER ON THE ROAD

1. "Leprosy," *Bible History Online,* http://www.bible- history.com/ backd2/leprosy.html, accessed 25 July 2016.

2. "Prejudice," http://www.thefreedictionary.com/, accessed 25 July 2016.

3. "Bigot," http://www.thefreedictionary.com/, accessed 25 July 2016.

4. "Discrimination," http://www.thefreedictionary.com/, accessed 25 July 2016.

5. "Racism," http://www.thefreedictionary.com/, accessed 25 July 2016.

CHAPTER 8: KINGDOM BUILDING

1. "Kingdom"/*basileía,* Strong's #932, http://www.studylight.org/ lexicons/greek/gwview.cgi?n=932, accessed 25 July 2016.

2. "God"/*theós,* Strong's #2316, http://www.studylight.org/lexi-cons/greek/gwview.cgi?n=2316, accessed 25 July 2016.

ABOUT THE AUTHOR

CHARLIE TUTTLE AND his wife, Sherri, have pastored Genesis Church in McKinney, TX, since 2002. Charlie and Sherri have three incredible adult children, Gentry, Weston, and Payton, who work and minister along-side them. Sherri is an ovarian cancer survivor who refuses to give up or surrender her life to disease. Charlie is a passionate speaker, writer, and developer of people. Charlie enjoys golf, Tex-Mex food, and watching Texas sunsets with Sherri.

CONTACT THE AUTHOR

CHARLIE TUTTLE CAN be contacted at charlie@
charlietuttle.org or by mail. His mailing address
is 5780 Virginia Parkway, McKinney, TX 75071.
His Website is www.charlietuttle.org. Follow him on
Twitter at @ctutt3 or find him on Facebook.